Esther

INTERPRETATION

A Bible Commentary for Teaching and Preaching

INTERPRETATION
A BIBLE COMMENTARY FOR TEACHING AND PREACHING

James Luther Mays, *Series Editor*
Patrick D. Miller, *Old Testament Editor*
Paul J. Achtemeier, *New Testament Editor*

CAROL M. BECHTEL

Esther

INTERPRETATION

A Bible Commentary
for Teaching and Preaching

John Knox Press
LOUISVILLE

For
Andrew and Ellen

Library of Congress Cataloging-in-Publication Data

Bechtel, Carol M., 1959–
    Esther / Carol M. Bechtel.
        p. cm. — (Interpretation, a Bible commentary for teaching and preaching)
    Includes bibliographical references.
    ISBN 0-8042-3113-3 (alk. paper)
    1. Bible. O.T. Esther—Commentaries.   I. Title.   II. Series.

  BS1375.3 .B43 2001
  222'.907—dc21   2001056760

© copyright Carol M. Bechtel 2002
This book is printed on acid-free paper that meets the American National Standards Institute Z39.48 standard. ∞
02 03 04 05 06 07 08 09 10 11 — 10 9 8 7 6 5 4 3 2 1
Printed in the United States of America
John Knox Press
Louisville, Kentucky

SERIES PREFACE

This series of commentaries offers an interpretation of the books of the Bible. It is designed to meet the need of students, teachers, ministers, and priests for a contemporary expository commentary. These volumes will not replace the historical critical commentary or homiletical aids to preaching. The purpose of this series is rather to provide a third kind of resource, a commentary which presents the integrated result of historical and theological work with the biblical text.

An interpretation in the full sense of the term involves a text, an interpreter, and someone for whom the interpretation is made. Here, the text is what stands written in the Bible in its full identity as literature from the time of "the prophets and apostles," the literature which is read to inform, inspire, and guide the life of faith. The interpreters are scholars who seek to create an interpretation which is both faithful to the text and useful to the church. The series is written for those who teach, preach, and study the Bible in the community of faith.

The comment generally takes the form of expository essays. It is planned and written in the light of the needs and questions which arise in the use of the Bible as Holy Scripture. The insights and results of contemporary scholarly research are used for the sake of the exposition. The commentators write as exegetes and theologians. The task which they undertake is both to deal with what the texts say and to discern their meaning for faith and life. The exposition is the unified work of one interpreter.

The text on which the comment is based is the Revised Standard Version of the Bible and, since its appearance, the New Revised Standard Version. The general availability of these translations makes the printing of a text in the commentary unnecessary. The commentators have also had other current versions in view as they worked and refer to their readings where it is helpful. The text is divided into sections appropriate to the particular book; comment deals with passages as a whole, rather than proceeding word by word, or verse by verse.

Writers have planned their volumes in light of the requirements set by the exposition of the book assigned to them. Biblical books differ in character, content, and arrangement. They also differ in the way they have been and are used in the liturgy, thought, and devotion of the church. The distinctiveness and use of particular books have been taken into account in decisions about the approach, emphasis, and use of space in the commentaries. The goal has been to allow writers to develop the format which provides for the best presentation of their interpretation.

The result, writers and editors hope, is a commentary which both explains and applies, an interpretation which deals with both the meaning and the significance of biblical texts. Each commentary reflects, of course, the writer's own approach and perception of the church and world. It could and should not be otherwise. Every interpretation of any kind is individual in that sense; it is one reading of the text. But all who work at the interpretation of Scripture in the church need the help and stimulation of a colleague's reading and understanding of the text. If these volumes serve and encourage interpretation in that way, their preparation and publication will realize their purpose.

The Editors

ACKNOWLEDGMENTS

Not long ago I happened upon the English Bible I had used as a child (a red-letter edition King James, no less). I opened it to the book of Esther and was surprised when several dried flower petals fell out. Evidently I had thought Esther would be a good place to press them, since I did not plan to read it very much. Fortunately, those plans were foiled.

I am grateful, first, to James L. Mays for inviting me to write for this series. It is the one I always recommend to my seminary students and give to my friends. I am grateful to both Professor Mays and Patrick Miller for their patient and expert editorial guidance. Thanks, as well, to President Dennis Voskuil, Dean James Brownson, my secretary Judy Bos, and all my colleagues at Western Theological Seminary for their support and encouragement on this project.

My students have taught me more about the book of Esther than anyone. I am grateful to all of them, but some of them deserve special mention. Regina Plunkett, Rebecca Stegeman Riekse, and Peg Atkinson each contributed in diverse manners, some of which they probably do not even remember. Also important were all the people in small churches across West Michigan who came to class simply because they love the Bible and often set me straight about what the book of Esther is "really about." I am especially grateful to the congregations of Haven Reformed, Maplewood Reformed, and First Reformed, Grand Haven.

Finally, I need to thank my family and friends. I am grateful to my parents, Glenn and Rhea Bechtel, for their faith in both God and me, and for letting me read the Bible in church when the sermons got boring. Thanks to the choir at Third Reformed Church for not giving my choir robe away when I skipped practice to work on this book. Thanks to Leanne VanDyk and Tom Mullens for conspiring to keep my spirits up. And finally, thanks to my children, Andrew and Ellen, who will never know how much they contributed to this commentary. I have been working on it for almost half their lives. It is dedicated to them.

Pentecost, 2001

CONTENTS

INTERPRETATION

Introduction

Soon after historian Deborah Lipstadt won a court victory over Holocaust denier David Irving, she went to hear the scroll of Esther read at her local synagogue's celebration of Purim. When she heard the words from Esther 4:14—"Who knows? Perhaps you have come to royal dignity for just such a time as this," she listened in light of her recent experience. "I heard that," she said,

> and it made me think: Who knows if not for this very reason I got the education I got, I got the upbringing I got, my job—maybe we're all meant to do one something really significant. And some of us do it on the public stage, and some do it by helping a child. Nobody knows of it, nobody sees it, but we're all meant to do something. And maybe this is the something I was meant to do. (*The Jerusalem Post Magazine*, June 2, 2000, p. 16)

Lipstadt's moment in history's limelight was unusual, but her reaction to the book of Esther was not. People of faith (both Jews and Christians) have been reading this book for millennia and reacting in similar ways. Something about this book makes us all take stock of ourselves and wonder what God is up to. Something about this book makes us laugh and cry and thank God all at the same time.

This commentary is intended to aid and abet that process, both for individuals and for faith communities. Whether we are considering the "vital statistics" of the book's character and composition or reveling in the story's own delightful moments, the assumption is the same: that God has given us the book of Esther "for just such a time as this."

Vital Statistics

1. Versions of Esther

The first question that confronts interpreters of the book of Esther is: *Which* book of Esther? Or perhaps more properly: *Whose* book of Esther?

Jews and Protestants share a version of the book that is based on the Masoretic Text (MT), a Hebrew version that has been passed down by the rabbis and is regarded as canonical by both faith communities. Eastern Orthodox and Roman Catholic Christians, on the other hand, include a different version of Esther in their canons. It is based on the

Greek Septuagint (LXX), a translation of a Hebrew original that differs from the MT in some respects. Most of these differences are relatively minor. There is, however, one major discrepancy where the book of Esther is concerned: The Septuagint includes six passages that are not in the MT (107 verses in all).

Understanding the different canonical manifestations of these additions requires a short—but fascinating—course in church history. When the fourth-century church father Jerome set about translating the Bible into Latin (now known as the Vulgate), he was troubled by the fact that he could find no Hebrew manuscripts for these six additions. So he placed them at the end of his translation of the book of Esther. When the Protestant Reformers set about shaping their version of the canon in the sixteenth century, they followed Jerome's lead, but removed them one step further from the rest of the book by transferring them to the Apocrypha (that group of books between the testaments that are considered edifying reading, but not "Scripture" per se).

The Roman Catholic community responded to such Protestant innovations at the Council of Trent (1545–63). One of the many decisions to come out of this council was to reaffirm the canonical status of the Apocryphal (or deuterocanonical) books, including these six "Additions to Esther." Eastern Orthodox Christians also regard them as canonical. Practices vary as to whether the "additions" are printed separately or as integrated parts of the rest of the book of Esther.

The challenges posed for the interpreter by these two main manifestations of Esther are obvious. Each canonical version has its own integrity within the faith community that holds it dear. As a Protestant Christian, however, I am hesitant to think that I could do justice to both. Yet to ignore the additions completely seems both arrogant and unecumenical. The approach taken in this commentary, therefore, is intended as a kind of compromise. The main commentary is based on the MT. The additions are considered below in the Appendix, though every effort will be made there to interpret them within the context of the book as a whole. I hope that this will make it possible for people of all three Christian traditions to use the commentary. It is striking how differently the book reads with and without the additions. I hope that an awareness of these differences will lead to mutual appreciation and understanding rather than the reverse. A common commitment to interpreting the Bible for the church will surely be the similarity that overshadows such differences.

2. Date and Historicity

2

The book of Esther is set during the reign of the Persian king Ahasuerus (Xerxes I), who ruled from 486 to 465 B.C.E. Several things suggest that it was written later, however, not the least of which is the opening phrase to the book of Esther: "This happened in the days of Ahasuerus," which implies a perspective after the fact. While the author uses several Persian loan words and many authentic Persian names, and seems to have a fair acquaintance with Persian customs (such as the Persian pony express), his knowledge of precise historical detail for the period about which he writes is a bit uncertain. More will be said in a moment about these details. Further, the book's Hebrew has much in common with other "late Hebrew" biblical books such as Ezra, Nehemiah, and Chronicles, which are usually dated at around 400–300 B.C.E. These clues combine, then, to argue that the book of Esther was written at least eighty years after the time it describes.

The *terminus ad quem* is usually fixed at the rise of the Seleucid dynasty during the Greek period (200 B.C.E.). This was the time when the Greek rulers took a considerably more antagonistic approach to their conquered subjects, a policy that eventually gave rise to the Maccabean Revolt (167 B.C.E.). While the Jews of the book of Esther are under threat, that threat has more to do with temporary personal antagonism than permanent national policy. Furthermore, the book's own attitude toward foreign rulers tends more toward accommodation than does the literature from this later period. In light of these considerations, most scholars today date the book to sometime between the years 400 and 200 B.C.E., that is, in the late Persian or early Greek period.

As the above reflections already suggest, there is some reason to doubt the historicity of the book of Esther. We know from extrabiblical sources, for instance, that Xerxes I was off fighting the Battle of Salamis at the time when, according to the book, Esther was brought into the harem (2:16; 480 B.C.E.). The Greek historian Herodotus reports that, for at least several months after that famous battle, the king was involved in a disastrous dalliance with his daughter-in-law (Herodotus IX 108–13). Also, we know that his queen was named Amestris and that she probably came from one of the seven noble families of Persia (Herodotus III 84; VII 114; IX 108–13). Although Herodotus can hardly be called impartial (the Greeks and the Persians were enemies, after all), he would hardly have made up the king's role in the battle of Salamis, nor the identity of his longtime queen.

There are other details that do not ring true. Much is made in the book of the king's "one hundred twenty-seven provinces" (1:1; 8:9; 9:30). Other ancient sources know of far fewer, with estimates ranging from twenty to thirty. Also suspect is the notion that Persian laws could not be modified or revoked. The only places in ancient literature where this is claimed are in Esther 8 (and perhaps 1:19, though see

3

commentary, p. 71–72) and Daniel 6. In both these biblical books the "rule" may be more a function of the plot than of actual historical practice. Finally, one has to wonder about some of the improbable statistics in the book: a 180-day drinking bash for the entire army (1:3–4), the 75-foot gallows/stake that Haman erected in his back yard (5:14), and the 75,000-person death toll in the provinces (9:16).

What are we to make of this? How can this long list of historical inaccuracies and logical improbabilities be reconciled with this author's often "realistic" descriptions of Persian language and culture? More important for communities of faith, how does this lack of historicity affect our sense of this book's being the Word of God? Both of these questions can perhaps best be dealt with in a discussion of the book's form.

3. Form and Structure

There is every evidence that this author was not trying to write "history" in the sense that modern people think of that word. Thus, attempts to force this book into that mold may actually do its author an injustice. But if not history, then what?

Many educated guesses have been made as to the genre of the book of Esther. Some of the chief proposals are: wisdom tale, historical novella/romance, literary carnival tale, short story, and Diaspora novel. (For these and others, see Fox, 141–52.) What all of these suggestions have in common is a certain basic element of fictionality. In using this term we should be careful not to equate fiction with untruth. To understand this, one only has to think of how truth manifests itself in any great work of fiction. Charles Dickens tells a great deal of truth, for instance, in his classic story *A Christmas Carol*. While many of its details are historically accurate, the story never sets out to be a chronicle of nineteenth-century England. Fiction, then, is not the *absence* of truth, but often the *vehicle* for it. Historical fiction, while drawing on both the outlines and details of history, is still intended to tell a truth that goes beyond historical accuracy.

One of the most fruitful suggestions on the kind of literature Esther is comes from Adele Berlin, who identifies it as a "burlesque." That is, it is a kind of literary caricature or farce that can take on a tone of "mock dignity," often with hilarious results (Berlin, xvi–xxii). This style employs the following: "exaggeration, caricature, ludicrous situations, practical jokes, coincidences, improbabilities, and verbal humor . . . repetition—of scenes, events, and phrases—and inversions or reversals" (xix). It is easy to see how this style applies to Esther, though with the proviso that humor can sometimes convey quite serious points. In Esther we laugh until we cry.

4

Berlin's theory has obvious implications for the way one reads the story. Not only does it change one's expectations rather dramatically, but in doing so, it may also be considerably more fair to the story the author is trying to tell. In Berlin's words, "The largest interpretive problems melt away if the story is taken as a farce or a comedy associated with a carnival-like festival" (xxii). The only mystery is why it took us so long to realize this, given that the book is traditionally read at the carnival-like festival of Purim.

Once free of the question of the book's genre, we are in a better position to appreciate the literary artistry of this story. One of the ways this manifests itself is in the book's structure.

Many have noticed the frequency of *banquets* or *feasts* in this story (both words are translations of the Hebrew word *mišteh*). Few have appreciated their structural significance as well as Michael V. Fox, however (Fox, p. 157; also reproduced in Levenson, 5). The following diagram charts the correspondences Fox identifies between and among the ten banquets described in the book:

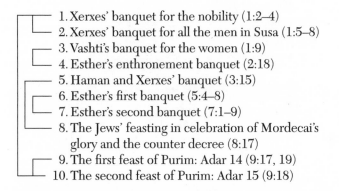

1. Xerxes' banquet for the nobility (1:2–4)
2. Xerxes' banquet for all the men in Susa (1:5–8)
3. Vashti's banquet for the women (1:9)
4. Esther's enthronement banquet (2:18)
5. Haman and Xerxes' banquet (3:15)
6. Esther's first banquet (5:4–8)
7. Esther's second banquet (7:1–9)
8. The Jews' feasting in celebration of Mordecai's glory and the counter decree (8:17)
9. The first feast of Purim: Adar 14 (9:17, 19)
10. The second feast of Purim: Adar 15 (9:18)

While correspondences are not always completely symmetrical (3 and 4, for instance, have no real counterparts between 8 and 9), they are striking enough to suggest that at least the final editor of the book intended to create them. It can hardly be an accident that a book whose final form is designed to perpetuate the two-day feast of Purim should be structured around "ten banquets—that is, five sets of two" (Levenson, 6).

One of the things this analysis begins to highlight is contrasts, or more properly, reversals. The Persian feasts of 1 and 2 are in contrast with the Purim feasts of 9 and 10. The banquet that culminates in Vashti's demotion as queen (3) is in contrast with the banquet that celebrates Esther's coronation as queen (4). Haman and Xerxes lift their glasses to celebrate the first decree (5), and the Jews lift their glasses to celebrate the second one (8).

There is a sense in which the whole book of Esther could be summed up in two Hebrew words from 9:1—*nahăpôk hû*—"the reverse occurred" (Brooks Schramm in Levenson, 8). Levenson illustrates this graphically in a chart that highlights the book's great reversals (Levenson, 8):

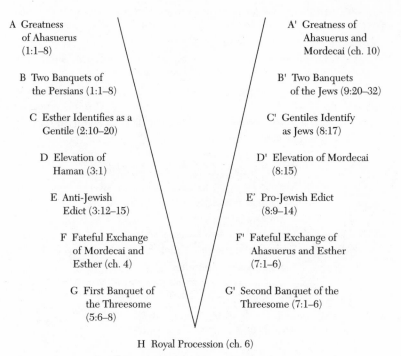

A Greatness
   of Ahasuerus
   (1:1–8)

  B Two Banquets of
     the Persians (1:1–8)

    C Esther Identifies as a
       Gentile (2:10–20)

      D Elevation of
        Haman (3:1)

        E Anti-Jewish
          Edict (3:12–15)

          F Fateful Exchange
             of Mordecai and
             Esther (ch. 4)

             G First Banquet of
               the Threesome
               (5:6–8)

A' Greatness of
    Ahasuerus and
    Mordecai (ch. 10)

B' Two Banquets
    of the Jews (9:20–32)

C' Gentiles Identify
   as Jews (8:17)

D' Elevation of Mordecai
   (8:15)

E' Pro-Jewish Edict
   (8:9–14)

F' Fateful Exchange of
   Ahasuerus and Esther
   (7:1–6)

G' Second Banquet of the
   Threesome (7:1–6)

H Royal Procession (ch. 6)

Notice particularly the negative character of the events on the left side of the chart, and the positive character of the events on the right. The real strength of this structural analysis, however, is in the way it highlights the "pivot" of the book's plot, namely, chapter 6 (Levenson, 7). This, of course, is the chapter where Haman's hopes are dashed and Mordecai's fortunes begin to take a turn for the better. The words of Haman's wife and friends describe this turning point precisely: "If Mordecai, before whom your downfall has begun, is of the Jewish people, you will not prevail against him, but will surely fall before him" (6:13).

Recent attention to structural patterns has called into question some of the double- (or even triple-) source theories about the book that have been suggested by some earlier scholars (Bickerman, Bardtke, Cazelles, Clines, and Lebram). According to Bickerman, for instance, there are two plots. One revolves around Esther and her troubles with an evil vizier; the other revolves around Mordecai and his troubles with an evil vizier. The present story, in his view, "has two heroes and two plots, but the villain is the same in both" (Bickerman, 172). As interesting as this is from a developmental point of view, it probably misunderstands parallels as duplications. It also tends to discount the possibility—which would have been very real in this late period—that the book is a self-conscious literary creation. (This is true even if one recognizes 9:20ff. as the work of a final editor.) The book's own preoccupation with the power of the written word (see below, pp. 14–16) bears this out.

Questions of genre and structure are fascinating for their own sakes, and are implicitly theological by virtue of the fact that they seek to appreciate the beauty of a literary creation. (Authors reflect the fact that they are created in the image of God every time they create a work of literature.) Yet these questions also prepare the way for us to consider some themes that are more explicitly theological. To those themes we now turn.

Theological Themes

1. The Importance of Proportion

A healthy sense of proportion is one of the things that distinguishes the wise from the foolish in the Bible's wisdom literature. Although Talmon's attempts to describe the entire book of Esther as a wisdom tale are probably a bit forced (see Fox, 142–43), this particular motif does reflect wisdom's concerns.

That proportion is a value for Esther's author is obvious from our brief look at the book's structure. Parallels abound as one element after another is balanced with its counterpart as on two sides of a scale. That this value should manifest itself in the book's content can hardly come as a surprise.

Our first clue to the importance of this theme comes in the opening chapter. Ahasuerus throws a 180-day drinking bout for the entire army, designed to display "the great wealth of his kingdom and the splendor and pomp of his majesty" (v. 4). Evidently his majesty's splendor continues to spill over even after six months, since a seven-day bash in the city of Susa follows. Here, the author treats us to sumptuous descriptions of the palace decor, and emphasizes the fact that "the royal wine was lavished according to the bounty of the king" with drinking "by flagons, without restraint" (vv. 7–8). While a more extensive discussion

7

of this scene will have to wait, what seems clear at the outset is that Ahasuerus does not do things by halves. This is a party of massive proportions. In fact, its scale is so grand as to strain credulity.

More important for the present discussion, however, is not the scale of the celebration but its lack of proportion. The party, remember, is designed to display the king's power. Yet the display climaxes with his very public embarrassment at the hands of Queen Vashti, who refuses to come when called. In one bold stroke, Vashti single-handedly exposes the mighty Ahasuerus for the weak, ineffectual man that he is (at least by ancient standards). He may command the entire army of Persia and Media and rule over "one hundred and twenty-seven provinces from India to Ethiopia" (v. 1), but he cannot control his own wife. Although Vashti's refusal falls short of other stories that describe the ultimate insult in the ancient world, namely, death at the hands of a woman (Judg. 4–5; 9:50–57; 2 Sam. 11:21), it is still in the same vein. In any case, her action reveals that Ahasuerus's earlier displays are badly out of proportion to his actual power.

Once we are alerted to the theme of proportion, we can begin to see its importance both in and among the characters.

Ahasuerus introduces us to the Persian proclivity for disproportion. Yet the 187 consecutive days of drinking are only the first of his many excesses. While the following list is not exhaustive, it is at least representative. It takes seven eunuchs to fetch Queen Vashti in 1:10 (though even they could not get the job done). Seven lawyers are required to decide what to do about her disobedience (1:13–14). All the beautiful young virgins of the empire are herded into the harem so that the king can choose one to be queen (2:1–4). An entire year is required to ready them for one night in the royal bedroom (2:12). The royal signet ring is passed around with a freedom that shows hardly any regard for the power it gives to the one who wears it. Finally, the most powerful man in the empire is powerless to revoke a law he was tricked into passing.

If we are impressed (or unimpressed) with Ahasuerus, however, it is only because we have not yet considered Haman. Haman's gift for disproportion makes Ahasuerus look like an amateur. When one man refuses to bow down, he is not content to punish him, but plots to kill him . . . with his entire race thrown in for good measure (3:5–6)! The bribe he offers Ahasuerus in pursuit of his goal is the equivalent of two-thirds of Persia's annual income (Beal, 53). (However, it could be argued that this absurd sum is *in proportion* with Haman's disproportionate rage.) His edict orders patriotic Persians not "only" to kill the Jews, but "to destroy, to kill, and to annihilate" them, "young and old,

8

women and children," and "to plunder their goods" (3:13). Finally, the gallows (or stake; see commentary, p. 55) Haman erects for Mordecai's execution is fully the height of a modern six-story building (5:14).

In contrast, especially to Haman, Esther emerges as the epitome of proportion. When given the opportunity to take whatever she wants for her one night with the king, she asks "for nothing except what Hegai the king's eunuch . . . advised" (2:13, 15). Upon hearing of the plot to assassinate Ahasuerus, she reacts with appropriate dispatch to save his life, but is careful to give Mordecai the credit for discovering the plot (2:22). She prepares for her momentous uninvited interview with the king by ordering a three-day fast, an act that is in stark contrast to the book's other banquets, but is completely appropriate to the serious nature of her mission (4:16). When the moment finally arrives for her to plead for the lives of her people, she matches Haman's rhetoric word for word, unmasking his deceit with her own modesty (7:1–6). When her request for the revocation of Haman's edict is denied, she and Mordecai draft a counteredict that is dictated by Haman's own extremes (8:8–14). (If anything, it falls short of them, thereby exemplifying another virtue of wisdom: restraint.) Finally, even Esther's request for an extension of the counteredict within the city of Susa is in proportion to the degree of hatred that still evidently prevailed against the Jews there (9:13–15).

The only character difficult to "grade" with regard to proportion is Mordecai. At issue is his refusal to bow to Haman in chapter 3. Although some background about a simmering feud between the house of Agag and the house of Benjamin may fill in the blanks a bit (see the commentary), it is hardly in the foreground of the text. This is almost certainly why other explanations have been sought (the LXX's Addition C has Mordecai refusing to bow to anyone but God; targumic and midrashic traditions actually suggest that Haman wore an idol on his chest). Regardless of the reasons for Mordecai's refusal, however, it should be pointed out that while his perpetual refusal to bow may be slightly out of proportion to the situation, it only seems so in light of the disproportionate dimensions of Haman's reaction. In other words, if Mordecai had known he was endangering the lives of his entire people, he might have acted differently. In any case, the story subsequently takes great delight in seeing Mordecai honored in proportion to his merits (6:10–11; 8:2).

Some interesting correspondences emerge when the characters are considered in this light. Not surprisingly, the correspondences themselves display a certain sensitivity to proportion.

Esther and Haman are clear counterparts. Indeed, much of the book's suspense revolves around whether any other character will arise

with the strength to counter his capacity for evil. Mordecai and Ahasuerus are a less obvious match, but both do display a certain ambiguity
of character in this category. While Ahasuerus displays the Persian penchant for disproportion, he doesn't really "mean anything by it." It turns
out badly only because he is such an easy target for Haman's manipulation. Similarly, Mordecai does not intend to doom his people by his
refusal to bow, but thanks again to Haman, his action has that effect.

Preachers in search of positive examples may find this analysis of
proportion in the book of Esther especially instructive (not to mention
the compelling negative examples this book affords!). One thing that
the analysis precludes, however, is making Mordecai the main hero of
the book. Carey Moore merely steps in line behind a long tradition of
commentators when he claims that "between Mordecai and Esther the
greater hero in the Hebrew is Mordecai, who supplied the brains while
Esther simply followed his directions. . . ." (Moore, *Esther*, LII). On the
contrary, it is Mordecai who—however unwittingly—gets the people of
God into this mess. It is left to Esther—with a lot of help from God and
a little help from Mordecai—to get them out.

2. The Challenge of Living a Faithful Life in an Unfaithful Culture

It is one thing to live a life that is faithful to God when one is surrounded by a culture that supports such efforts. It is quite another to
remain faithful in a cultural context that is not similarly committed and
that, in fact, may be openly hostile to the life of faith.

This is not news to Christians who live in places where persecution
is a constant companion. It may well be news, however, to Christians
who find themselves more and more the minority in a cultural context
that shares fewer and fewer of their values. North American Christians,
for instance, must deal daily with the tensions that arise between the
Gospel and an aggressively individualistic, consumeristic culture. How
do we live faithfully within this tension? Do we deny that there is any
tension and simply "become like the nations"? Do we heighten it and
attempt to cut ourselves off from all contact with outside influence? Or
do we seek some sort of critical compromise, adapting to our culture
wherever possible while still straining to maintain the integrity of faith?

There is a sense in which the book of Esther is an extended meditation on these very questions. Author Sidnie Ann White alerts us to this
possibility when she suggests that, while "the tale clearly is meant to
entertain . . . it has a didactic purpose as well," namely, "to teach Jews
how to live a productive life in the Diaspora" (White, 164). It is not hard
to imagine ways in which it might serve a similar function for modern

10

Christians as well. Indeed, it may be that the book of Esther has come to our attention for "just such a time as this" (4:14).

The one unalterable fact of life for the Jews in the book of Esther is *limited power*. While they may rise to some prominence (Mordecai, after all, is a courtier who sits at the king's gate), they are still not the ones who are in control of the situation. This is also evident in other books written in or about such contexts: Ezra/Nehemiah, Daniel 1–6, and the Joseph stories of Genesis 37–50.

For readers who have gone canoeing, the situation could be compared to trying to steer from the front of the canoe. It *can* be done, but only with a lot of exhausting effort, and even then, not always successfully. Esther and Mordecai spend the entire book trying to steer from the front of the canoe. Even when Esther is crowned queen and Mordecai is made the king's right-hand man, they must still reach and struggle even to stay upright, much less to get where they want to go.

The book itself does several things to underscore this theme of limited control. One of the primary places we encounter it is in 2:5–11. This is the passage that introduces Esther and Mordecai as the descendants of those carried off into exile by the Babylonians; it also describes the way Esther and the other young women are carried off to the king's harem. The passage is replete with passive verbs, a fact that is even more obvious in the wake of all the active verbs of 2:1–4, where Ahasuerus and his valets plan the roundup. By the end of verse 11, it is clear that Esther is doubly exiled and, thus, doubly vulnerable. This double dose of vulnerability does not necessarily translate into complete helplessness, however. Two other examples of characters with limited control serve both to illustrate this and to point out two possible methods of "steering from the front."

The character of Vashti has long fascinated feminists and frightened misogynists. Although she makes only a brief appearance in the first chapter, it is long enough to be instructive. She may be queen, but she is still a woman in the midst of a patriarchal culture, and thus has limited control over her situation. This is made pointedly obvious when Ahasuerus calls her to make an appearance at the men's banquet. The narrative does not speculate about either her options or her motives. It simply tells us that she refuses to go. It is hard not to admire her courage, even while one recognizes that it costs her dearly. Both her action and the king's reaction illustrate the dangers of an uncompromising approach to a situation of limited power, however. Resistance feels great for a moment (and in some situations, it may be the only choice), but the consequences can be dire.

Vashti's "approach" serves as an important foil for Esther's as the plot progresses. In contrast to Vashti's outright rejection of the status

11

quo, Esther opts for critical compromise. (Whether she is herself "compromised" by this approach has been the subject of centuries of debate.) Inasmuch as possible, she adapts to the prevalent culture. Yet she prepares to die if and when that stance no longer becomes possible (4:16). In the meantime she does her best to play the system against the system—using her position as queen to influence Ahasuerus, using her considerable intelligence to outwit Haman, and using Persian law to counteract Persian law.

Mordecai's stance actually has much in common with Vashti's at times. He, too, opts for a rigid and uncompromising response when confronted with the command to bow down to Haman (3:2). Sidnie Ann White points out that in doing so, "Mordecai is refusing to accept and work with his subordinate position" (169). While we have to admire his resolve, we have to wonder about his wisdom, especially given the way things work out. Mordecai's outright refusal to keep on "steering from the front" almost capsizes the canoe entirely. As Vashti's rash response resulted in a restrictive edict for all the women of Persia, so Mordecai's rash response *nearly* results in the death of all the Jews in Persia. The only reason it does not is because of the intervention of Esther—the character who is willing to entertain a more flexible approach to exile.

To be fair to Mordecai, however, we ought to recognize that he is not consistently uncompromising. He is the one who orders Esther to hide her identity as a Jew when she is taken into the harem. He also makes his living as a civil servant in the Persian court, and actually saves the life of the king by discovering the assassination plot (2:21–23). Thus, Mordecai's character is not completely parallel to either Vashti or Esther. In many ways his most complete parallel is outside the story— that is, with those of us who struggle with varying degrees of success to live in tension with our culture.

There is another character—or group of characters—who model this attempt to live life within limits. Although they are largely ignored in most commentaries, eunuchs play a significant role in the story, and are perhaps best discussed in this context. Eunuchs are expressly mentioned (often by name) in nine separate passages: 1:10–11; 1:15; 2:3; 2:8–11; 2:14; 2:15; 2:21; 4:4; 4:5–17; 6:2; 6:14; and 7:9. They seem to be everywhere: carrying messages, escorting characters, guarding the harem. Their presence is crucial to the outcome of the story in several instances. Most of these "interventions" are positive, such as Hegai's favor and advice in 2:9 and 15, or Harbona's timely suggestion in 7:9. In the one instance where their role is portrayed in a negative light (Bigthan and Teresh's foiled assassination attempt in 2:21–23), the inci-

12

dent sets up two important positives, namely Mordecai's saving the king (2:22) and his eventual promotion (6:1–11).

If the one unalterable fact of life for the Jews in the book of Esther is limited power, then the parallels between the Jews and the book's ubiquitous eunuchs are obvious. They, too, are in a condition of proscribed limits that they did not choose, forced to make the best of a situation that is less than ideal. What power they have they derive from considerable effort. What choices they have derive from the degree to which they are willing to accommodate. Bigthan and Teresh choose open rebellion and, like Vashti, pay dearly for it. Hegai and Harbona manage to get what they want by waiting for just the right moment to put a word in. In short, the eunuchs offer yet another example of how to negotiate life within limits. Fortunately for the book's protagonists, most of the eunuchs seem to be on their side. It is a logical alliance.

There is one other character in the book of Esther who keeps an even lower profile than the eunuchs, but who is even more important for the happy resolution of both Esther's story and our own. That character is: God.

Much has been made of the absence of God—or at least God's name—in the book of Esther. The standard explanation for this centers on the exuberant context of the Purim festival at which the scroll of Esther is read aloud, usually with enthusiastic audience participation. As drinking and feasting play a significant part in the story, so drinking and feasting often play a significant part in the celebration. According to the Talmud (Megilla 7b), one should drink enough so as not to be able to distinguish "cursed be Haman" from "blessed be Mordecai." While these instructions may make for a great party, they make for a risky reading, especially for those Jews afraid of violating the prohibition on pronouncing the name of God. Thus, the explanation goes, the name for God is left out as a precautionary measure.

Whether this explanation is fact or fiction, the absence of God's name does not necessarily imply the absence of God in the story. There is, of course, the mysterious reference to help arriving "from another quarter" in 4:14, which is often cited as an oblique reference to God. Yet this is by no means the only place God shows up in the book of Esther. In a manner quite similar to the stories of Joseph and Ruth, God's presence also is felt in the book's "coincidences" (see commentary, pp. 35, 39, 51–52, 57–58, 62, 65). The most prominent of these is in chapter 6, when the king's insomnia leads to his discovery of Mordecai's unrewarded loyalty. Arguably as important are any of the following:

the whole series of events that lead to Esther's being chosen as
queen

the lot's falling twelve month's hence (3:7)

Haman's entrance in the court just as Ahasuerus is trying to
think of a way to reward Mordecai (6:4)

the king's return from the garden at the precise moment that
Haman literally throws himself on Esther's mercy (7:8)

All of these so-called coincidences occur at critical junctures in the
story. Without them, the story would have a very different—and very
tragic—resolution.

All of this is to say that God is very much a character in this book,
though one who evidently prefers to remain anonymous. This should
be of considerable comfort to those of us who are struggling to remain
faithful in the midst of an unfaithful culture. Like the Jews, the women,
and the eunuchs in the book of Esther, we must make difficult decisions
about whether to adopt, reject, or adapt to our situation. Yet God is with
us in the midst of that struggle. We may wish at times that God's presence and power were a little more obvious. But as the incarnation itself
illustrates, even God sometimes chooses to steer from the front.

3. The Power of the Written Word

Seen from a slightly different angle, the book of Esther could also
be considered an extended meditation on the power of the written
word. The relevance of this theme for contemporary Christians will
become apparent.

That written texts are important in the book of Esther is obvious to
anyone who takes the time to count the references to them. There are
at least sixty-three references to writing or written texts in the book of
Esther. The following list indicates the specific Hebrew behind the
words or phrases that are included in this count:

"to write" (kātab)—24
"law/decree/edict" (dāt)—19
"letter/letter-writer" (sēper/sōpēr)—12
"copy" (patšegen)—3
"letter/missive" (ʾiggeret)—2
"annals" (dibrê hayyāmîn)—2
"decree" (pitgām)—1

14

That Esther's author was fascinated by the written word is obvious
from the above tally. What is less obvious is the significance of that fascination. One clue may come from the times in the book when the spo-

ken word is paired with the written word. Among these are instances when a verbal word (*dābār*) from the king is immediately followed by a reference to a written law (*dāt*), as in 1:19; 2:8; 4:3; and 9:1 (see also 9:14 and 9:32). When the book's three edicts are sent out, the publication is described in terms of both written script and spoken language (1:21; 3:12; and twice in 8:9). These references help us to narrow our focus, then, to the author's fascination with the relationship between written and spoken words. The question of significance has still to be determined.

When we look at the way written texts function in this story, the first thing that becomes apparent is their power. The "every man's home is his castle" edict in chapter 1 had a darkly oppressive edge to it that foreshadows edicts yet to come. Whether or not this particular edict is meant to be irrevocable is uncertain, but that Haman's edict in chapter 3 is understood this way is indisputable (8:8). This sets up a situation in which Haman's death-dealing words actually outlive him. Even after his nefarious plot is exposed and he is executed, the only way the Jews can fight back is with a counteredict (8:9ff.).

Although more extensive discussion of this will have to wait for the commentary itself, there is reason to believe that Haman's whole strategy revolves around this relationship between the written and the oral word. As we will argue on pp. 42–3, his spoken argument to Ahasuerus in 3:8–9 enjoys a level of ambiguity that the written version of the same does not (3:13). At the very least, the written version enjoys a powerful specificity and permanence that the spoken version cannot even approach. In the written edict the Jews are not only to be destroyed, but killed and annihilated as well. Their death sentence is dutifully translated into all the languages of the realm and sent with all dispatch to the far corners of the kingdom. Finally, it is sealed with the king's own ring, giving it an authority that even the king cannot later overrule.

One of the most overlooked texts in the book of Esther is the king's own book of days. These royal annals play a pivotal role when they are brought out in chapter 6 as a cure for the king's insomnia. In a wonderful stroke of irony, the servants "happen" to read aloud the story of Bigthan and Teresh's foiled conspiracy. Thus, the written record of the king's salvation through Mordecai becomes an instrument of Mordecai's own salvation. Thoughtful readers are left weak in the knees when we consider this doubly close call. If the king had not been "sleepless in Susa," and if the servants had not read that precise passage, Mordecai would have been hanged the very next morning and the whole story would have taken a terrible turn for the worse. The message here may serve as a kind of caveat. Even written texts lose their power when they remain unread. The process must come full circle: words are spoken,

15

words are written, and words are spoken aloud again. As long as the word goes unread, the truth will lie buried.

This truth seems to be at the heart of the written texts that are the focus of the book's ending. Two mass mailings are described in chapter 9, both designed to establish and perpetuate the celebration of Purim. The first set of letters is sent by Mordecai (9:20–23 and probably 9:26–28). Esther "seconds" this set with a mailing of her own (though it may have been jointly issued with Mordecai) in 9:29–32. The emphasis in both these letters and in the words that describe them is on remembering and keeping the story of their deliverance alive. What better way to do this than to read the written story aloud? This is exactly how the festival is celebrated to this day.

That an extended meditation on the power of the written word—and the importance of reading it—should arise in the postexilic period is not surprising. This was a time when the people of God sought to collect and edit what would become Scripture, and to redefine themselves as "a people of the book." What is surprising is that such an extended meditation should be so little used and so poorly understood among Christians. We also claim this book as Scripture, after all, and derive a significant part of our identity from being "a people of the book." Protestants particularly tout "Sola Scriptura!" as our rallying cry. More will be said about this Christian conundrum in a moment. For now, let it suffice to say that "every text is a dead letter unless the writer and the reader collaborate to keep it alive" (R. Plunkett, private communication). As long as Esther's word goes unread, its truth will lie buried.

Reading, Preaching, and Teaching the Book of Esther

1. Luther and the Lectionary

Christians have not always known what to do with the book of Esther. Sadly typical (and certainly influential) is Martin Luther's verdict. In *Table Talk*, he confessed that he wished the book did not exist at all, saying that it "Judaizes" too much and is full of "pagan naughtiness" (Bornkamm, 189).

Brutal as Luther is, he at least scores points for candor. It may also help to hear his comments in context. His medieval Christian predecessors relied heavily on allegorical and typological interpretations as their primary means for appropriating the book. Rhabanus Maurus, for instance, wrote a commentary on the book in the ninth century that aligns Esther with the church and Ahasuerus (!) with Christ. That Rhabanus's views were widespread is evidenced in medieval art, which depicted Esther as the "queen of heaven" and the "host of the messianic banquet" (Vrudny, 36).

Somewhere between these two extremes is a "more excellent way," though one wonders how to find it. One place to look might be the lectionary.

In the three-year cycle of the *Revised Common Lectionary*, the book of Esther is featured only once. Readings from Esther 7:1–6, 9–10 and 9:20–22 are listed with Psalm 124; James 5:13–20; and Mark 9:38–50 for Proper 21[26], in Year B. A brief look at these lections reveals a lot about one of the ways Christians seek—or don't seek—to appropriate Esther.

This lectionary is a widely used, ecumenical lectionary that was prepared by the Consultation on Common Texts, first in 1983 and then revised in 1992. Two "tracks" of readings are offered for Ordinary Time, that is, for the Sundays after Pentecost. One of these sets provides for a series of semicontinuous readings from the Old Testament and from non-Gospel New Testament texts. This was done in deference to the "long-standing and greatly loved tradition in Protestant churches of preaching which focuses entirely on the Old Testament or the epistle" (*RCL*, 15). Thus, the Old Testament readings in this track are not as closely aligned with the Gospel reading as they are in the other track or during the other seasons of the church year. Theoretically, then, this is the time when the lectionary allows the Old Testament to shine.

When we look at what this means for preaching Esther, however, we see that these few verses from Esther are sandwiched between three weeks of Proverbs and three weeks of Job. They are only internally "semi-continuous," then, and even so, the emphasis falls more on the "semi" than the "continuous." Esther 7:1–6 and 9–10 is the story of Esther's second banquet and Haman's exposure (minus the best part); 9:20–22 jumps ahead to Mordecai's letter and the establishment of Purim. The verses are, in short, little more than a sample.

The difficulties posed for the preacher here are obvious, especially in a context where we can no longer assume that the congregation already knows the story. When we remember that this reading comes up only once every three years (and even then will probably have to share the limelight with the other lections), one thing seems obvious: We cannot rely on the lectionary to acquaint our congregations with the book of Esther.

There is a sense in which the lectionary does not get us much beyond Luther, and one wonders whether some of Luther's negative biases are still a subconscious factor in our decisions. Could it be that one of the reasons we do not give the book of Esther more "airtime" is that we simply do not know what to say about it?

Once again, we must search for a more excellent way.

17

2. Total Immersion

Christians could take a lesson from Jews in how to appropriate the book of Esther. While I am not suggesting that we suddenly start celebrating Purim, that festival's use of the book/scroll of Esther is highly instructive.

First, the book is read in its entirety. This is really the only way to appreciate all of the reversals, ironies, and repetitions that suffuse this story. When we have just read how Mordecai saves Ahasuerus from the assassins at the end of chapter 2, for instance, we are in a position to be surprised that it is Haman who receives a promotion at the beginning of chapter 3. With Vashti's fate fresh in our minds, we can better appreciate the risk Esther runs when she goes to the king uninvited. We are also more likely to catch one of the book's best ironies: Vashti does not come when she is called—Esther comes when she is *not* called! These examples at least suggest the wisdom of reading the book from start to finish, preferably in one session.

Second, there is much to be said for reading the book aloud—and in community. One of the things that is more likely to come through in such a setting is the book's humor. George Eliot once said that the literature of the Old Testament "gives an idea of a people who went about their business and their pleasure as gravely as a society of beavers" (Radday, 21). Eliot's words are a caricature (of both the Bible and beavers!), but they reveal a presumption that is widespread especially among Protestants, namely, that the Bible cannot be humorous. The book of Esther is one of the Bible's best antidotes to such a presumption. Jewish commentator Adele Berlin revels in this when she writes that while "the threat of the destruction of the Jews is no laughing matter . . . the book of Esther is hilariously funny." In fact, she calls "the combination of a serious theme and a comic style" a "successful rhetorical strategy" (xvi).

Another thing that reading Esther aloud makes possible is interaction. By this I have more in mind than the usual cheers and boos for the various heroes and villains. Something about the story of Esther invites discussion. Some of the best opportunities, for instance, arise from the "ellipses" in the text. By this I am not referring to actual textual gaps, but a moment when a character's actions are described, but very little help is given with regard to their feelings or motivations. (What is Mordecai thinking, for instance, when he refuses to bow to Haman?) In the commentary I have tried to make the most of these moments, suggesting several possibilities without going further than the text itself warrants. Such "reading between the lines" takes self-control, lest one gets too far afield from what the Bible actually says. Yet these are often the moments when the characters' struggles most inform our own.

These same ellipses were seized on as opportunities in the Greek additions (see Appendix). Mordecai's prayer, for instance, in Addition C answers the question about his motives by saying, "I did this so that I might not set human glory above the glory of God, and I will not bow down to anyone but you, who are my Lord." It is instructive, then, to see the ways in which these additions seek to resolve the ambiguities in the Hebrew version. Readers who enjoy ambiguity may resent this; readers who do not may be relieved by it. In either case, the way others have chosen to "fill in the blank" will provide ample opportunity for discussion.

The lectionary may also lead us in this direction in its listing of Psalm 124 as a "response" to the Old Testament reading from Esther. In a manner very similar to the apocryphal additions, the psalm gives voice to a prayer appropriate to a people who have experienced sudden and miraculous deliverance.

> If it had not been the LORD who was on our side
> —let Israel now say—
> if it had not been the LORD who was on our side,
> when our enemies attacked us,
> then they would have swallowed us up alive,
> when their anger was kindled against us;
> then the flood would have swept us away,
> the torrent would have gone over us;
> then over us would have gone the raging waters.
> Blessed be the LORD,
> who has not given us as prey to their teeth.
> We have escaped like a bird from the snare of the fowlers;
> the snare is broken, and we have escaped.
> Our help is in the name of the LORD,
> who made heaven and earth.

The "interaction" that the lectionary suggests here leads us to a crucial issue for Christian appropriation of the book of Esther. When a Christian congregation responds to a reading from Esther with this prayer, we are doing more than celebrating someone else's deliverance—we are celebrating our own. This is not to minimize what the book of Esther or this psalm means to Jews—or to Christians who care about Jews. In a world familiar with the Holocaust (not to mention newscasts full of stories about contemporary genocides), we dare not ignore Haman's modern manifestations (even in ourselves) nor neglect to celebrate God's victory over them. Yet, when Christians pray Psalm 124 in a context like the one the lectionary suggests, we cannot help but recall the deliverance at the heart of our faith—Jesus Christ's victory over sin and death. In doing so, we may have more in common with the

19

Christian medieval interpreters than we first thought. (Though seeing Ahasuerus as a type for Christ still seems a bit of a stretch!)

In summary, then, Christians can learn much from the Jewish experience of the book of Esther. Much can be gained by: (1) reading the book in its entirety, (2) reading it aloud, and (3) reading it interactively. Finally, we should add a fourth learning: Much can be gained by *reading it repeatedly*.

Contemporary culture is fascinated by the "new." We value the spontaneous and worship the disposable. In such a context, repetition is at best confusing and at worst rejected. Still, there is something to be said for a long and loving relationship with a book like Esther. Its richness cannot possibly be appreciated in a single reading, but needs to be savored over several years and in several contexts. The book itself may stay the same, after all, but the readers will be in a different place each time they come to it. And there are not many places in life where we cannot afford to be reminded of God's providence and our responsibilities. As the book of Esther itself teaches us, a living word unread becomes a dead word. To that observation there is but one response: God save the queen!

PART ONE

ESTHER 1

Esther (1:1–9)
Pomp and Circumstance

The operative word in the first chapter of Esther is *excess*. We begin to suspect this in the very first verse. A king named Ahasuerus (literally "Mighty Man") is said to rule over one hundred twenty-seven provinces ranging from India to Ethiopia. (For a discussion of the historical identity of this king, see Introduction, p. 2–3). He sits, not simply on his throne, but on his *royal* throne (v. 2). His royal throne is located, not simply in the city of Susa, but in the citadel or acropolis of Susa. Whether one interprets this as a fortified compound or in more palatial terms, the sense still seems to be of an elite location.

This prime piece of real estate is then described as the setting for the lavish banquet (literally "drinking party") that the king hosts for "all his officials and ministers." The guest list burgeons almost beyond belief to include no less than "the army of Persia and Media and the nobles and governors of the provinces." Furthermore, the feast is said to last for a grand total of one hundred eighty days. It takes this much time, evidently, for the king to display the full extent of "the great wealth of his kingdom and the splendor and pomp of his majesty" (v. 4).

To be fair, we ought to pause at this point to ask a question: *Are we to understand this as excess or abundance?* Perhaps it is wrong to put a negative spin on what could be interpreted as a straightforward description of the grandeur of Ahasuerus's court.

One could make a case for abundance if it were not for the cumulative effect of the account. At every opportunity the author chooses the extravagant over the straightforward. The number of provinces is generally thought to be vastly exaggerated, since by all other accounts Persia had no more than thirty during this period (see Introduction, p. 3). The author is equally extravagant with words, never missing the opportunity for extra nouns and adjectives, especially if they have something to do with pomp and circumstance. (If nouns and adjectives had calories, the calorie count in verse 4 alone would be well over anyone's recommended daily allowance!) Finally, the author makes no attempt to mitigate the obviously absurd dimensions of the king's party. As commentator Jon Levenson rightly wonders, "Who was minding the store during this drinkfest of half a year's duration?" (45).

At first glance the author's style seems to imitate Ahasuerus's own "more is better" philosophy. Closer consideration, however, raises the question of whether the tone is not tongue in cheek. Are we really to believe that the author of the book of Esther did not see any logistical problems with a banquet of this size and scope? Are we really to believe that this author does not sense a certain absurdity in the over-the-top descriptions of Ahasuerus's splendor? Or is it possible that this author's tone is ironic, and therefore critical? Just because Ahasuerus is described in lavish terms does not necessarily imply the author's approval.

As suggested in the Introduction (pp. 4–5), an understanding of the book's form is crucial for making interpretive decisions about this book. Adele Berlin's suggestion that the book of Esther may actually be a "burlesque," that is, a kind of comic lampoon, is quite compelling (xix). She makes her case by way of a thorough review of other relevant literature from the ancient world, particularly Greek stories about the Persian court. Since the Greeks and the Persians were enemies during this period, one would hardly expect them to flatter Persian rulers. Just so, one would hardly expect a story written by Jews for Jews about their Persian overlords to be full of unmitigated admiration.

That the Bible should contain a lampoon of a foreign ruler is not a new idea. Other "obtuse foreign rulers" come to mind: Balak (Num. 22–24), Eglon (Judg. 3), and the Pharaoh of the Exodus stories (see Brenner, 42–51). These examples illustrate the varying degrees to which comedy comes into play, however. Even if we recognize some level of the burlesque in the book of Esther, it remains to be seen how fully it will play out with regard to the character of Ahasuerus. As we continue to read, we need at least to consider the possibility that Ahasuerus's splendor may be more than a little tarnished by the author's tone, and that what appears to be a characterization of abundance may, in fact, be a characterization of excess.

After one hundred eighty days we would expect both guests' appetites and the king's vanity to be sated. But verse 5 tells us that while the days were completed (literally "full"), the diners were not. Ahasuerus hosts yet another party, this time of seven days' duration. If the emphasis of the first banquet was quantity, the focus of the second is quality. Even the guest list is a kind of distillation of the larger population, with only the residents of the citadel of Susa being present. It is a garden party set in the court of the king's palace, with all manner of luxurious decorations set out especially for the occasion. Quality has not displaced quantity, however, for the "royal wine [is] lavished according to the bounty of the king" (v. 7). By this time we have formed a fairly definite impression of the scale of Ahasuerus's bounty. But the author does not risk leaving the details to our imagination. Drinking, we are told, is "by flagons, without restraint" (v. 8). Indeed, the king's only command is for self-command; he orders "all the officials of his palace to do as each one desire[s]" (v. 8).

The royal liberality even spills over to the ladies in waiting. Verse 9 notes that Queen Vashti also gives a banquet for the women of the palace. No further comment is made as to the nature of this gathering, but its mention may comment indirectly on the character of the king's banquet. While it was not uncommon for women and men to feast together in ancient Persia (see chapters 5 and 7 for examples), Ahasuerus's seven-day garden party is, apparently, "for men only." Or at least, the queen and the women of the court are not welcome. We can only speculate as to whether other women are present. As Levenson notes, "The absence of women at Ahasuerus's banquets enhances the perception that these were really just overdone 'stag parties,' with all the licentiousness and disrespect the term implies" (46).

Esther 1:10–21
Vashti Sparks a State Crisis

It hardly seems necessary for the author to tell us that the king's heart is "merry with wine" by the seventh day. Yet perhaps it goes to state of mind since in Hebrew the "heart" is the seat of both the emotions and the intellect. In fact, the heart is also the wellspring of the will, and Ahasuerus's merry heart "wills" Queen Vashti to come to the men's banquet wearing the royal crown. The author makes no secret of the king's motives: he wants to show her off (v. 10). Indeed, he has saved the best for last. Vashti is the prime piece of property that will "crown" his 187-day display. In the style of excess to which we have now become accustomed, he sends, not one, but seven eunuchs to fetch her.

There is only one problem: She won't come.

Wondering over the root of Vashti's disobedience, the rabbis suggest that perhaps Vashti is being ordered to wear *only* the royal crown here (Esther Rabbah III 13, p. 54; Pfisterer Darr, p. 169). Given the nature of the festivities to which she has been summoned, however, it seems unnecessary to speculate beyond the obvious. (Would *you* go?) In any case, the author does not seem especially interested in her rationale for refusing Ahasuerus's summons. No matter how curious we as readers are about Vashti, the narrative's focus is inexorably on Ahasuerus. The point to which the whole narrative builds is this: In spite of the king's immense wealth and power, he cannot control his own wife. One woman pulls the rug out from under the most powerful man in the world . . . and she does so while his whole world is watching.

Queen Vashti's refusal is a humiliation that is both public and absolute. (Imagine the unlucky eunuchs returning with the news!) Ahasuerus's rage literally "flames" forth. Seven sages are summoned to help Ahasuerus deal with the emergency. (Note the parallel to the seven eunuchs earlier in the chapter.) Whether these men are lawyers or astrologers is not clear. Modern rulers have demonstrated their dependence on both, and perhaps these men were some combination of the two. No matter what their exact credentials, however, the king obviously relies on them for advice. The fact that they are named adds to the gravity (mock gravity?) of the situation. In what is to be the first of several such incidents in the book, a personal or domestic dispute has mushroomed into a political crisis. No less than seven special prosecutors are required to arraign the recalcitrant queen and counsel the king on damage control.

Ahasuerus's question in verse 15 deserves specific comment. "According to the law," he asks, "what is to be done to Queen Vashti because she has not performed the command of King Ahasuerus conveyed by the eunuchs?" It seems odd that he does not know the laws of his own empire well enough to negotiate this fairly straightforward infraction. Further, the inclusion of the phrase "conveyed by the eunuchs" seems extraneous. Yet, since this chapter's theme centers on power versus powerlessness, the eunuchs may well be the author's way of underscoring Ahasuerus's own political impotence (see the Introduction, p. 12–13).

Memucan's advice in verses 16–20 comprises the largest block of direct speech in the chapter and, indeed, one of the largest in the book. On the one hand, it is a brilliant stroke of psychology. By interpreting Vashti's defiance as a crime against everyone in the empire, he deftly deflects the focus from the king. Suddenly, Ahasuerus is no longer the only man who is humiliated; every man in the realm is potentially vulnerable. In the space of a few sentences, Memucan manages to "take the heat off" Ahasuerus. On the other hand, one wonders if there is

24

more than diplomacy at work in Memucan's response. His nervous prediction of copycat crimes in every household may well reflect real male insecurity. Judging from the alacrity with which his proposals are lapped up by both the king and the other officials, one gets the impression that they are all genuinely frightened.

The scale of Memucan's suggestion is consistent with the pattern of excess we have already identified in the book. This time the excess is not in terms of possessions or power, but of action. One woman defies her husband. Suddenly there is a national crisis, and law is being rushed through the legislature. (As to whether this law is irrevocable, see p. 71–72.) Furthermore, this legislation is not limited to the one defiant woman, but is instead extended to every woman in the empire. Letters are sent "to all the royal provinces, to every province in its own script and to every people in its own language, declaring that every man should be master in his own house" (v. 22). How the legislators expected to enforce this sweeping command strains credulity. Excess everywhere abounds.

Irony is in plentiful supply as well. As a public relations strategy, Memucan's approach leaves a lot to be desired. Instead of confining the damage, the decree actually publicizes the king's humiliation. Memucan worries that "there will be no end of contempt and wrath" when the women of Persia and Media hear of the queen's behavior (v. 18). But the passage and publication of the decree virtually guarantees that they will hear of it, and in their own languages, no less! Carey Moore both concedes the irony and suggests an explanation for this. He writes, "that [Ahasuerus] should have brought into full play the communications system of the entire Persian Empire for such a purpose is ridiculous. Then again, drunken men sometimes are ridiculous" (*Esther,* 14).

There is a textual issue in verse 22. The Hebrew (MT) adds this phrase to the end of the verse: "and speak according to the language of his people." Although we have become accustomed to the ridiculous, this seems extreme even for Ahasuerus. Some scholars have explained it as a reference to the complications of communication that arose in international marriages (see Neh. 13:23ff.). The confusion is best resolved, however, by seeing this final phrase as a scribal error echoing the earlier reference to the languages of the various letters. It is significant that the phrase does not appear in the Septuagint (LXX). Thus, even though the notion of a law ordering every man to speak his own language at home seems almost as funny as one that commands every man to be master in his own house, we should probably make do with one less laugh.

The question of whether and how much to laugh is an important

25

one at this juncture. Even if one accepts the generally comic form of the book, there is a dark side to this edict that foreshadows other more serious edicts to come. This will not be the last time that an excess of pride and anger result in something that is oppressive. Even though this first edict is conceived in absurdity, it is born in cruelty. Women all over the Persian Empire will suffer for the arrogant extremes of Ahasuerus and his advisors. Perhaps the form of the burlesque blunts the pain, but there is a sense in which all of this book's humor is —sometimes literally—gallows humor. We not only laugh until we cry; we laugh so that we will not cry.

These observations are especially relevant for interpreting Ahasuerus's character. Berlin points out that he bears a striking resemblance to the stock character of the buffoon in Greek comedy (xx). While it is true that his "antics add an extra comic element," it is also true that Ahasuerus is a dangerous man. Some of his danger derives specifically from his absurdity. This is the man, after all, who is ostensibly in charge of the entire Persian Empire, and by extension, the fate of all the characters we care about. Esther's fear in approaching him later in the book is very real, as is the fearful result of his trust in Haman. Ahasuerus may not *mean* to do wicked and destructive things, but he does them nevertheless. (Intentionality is probably what sets him apart from Haman later in the story.) In short, Ahasuerus may be a buffoon . . . but he is a dangerous buffoon.

This example underscores, once more, how crucial it is to make some conscious decisions about this book's form before attempting to apply it to contemporary life. Preachers and teachers who vacillate are likely to send some very mixed and quite possibly dangerous messages.

Another example of a possible interpretive pitfall lies in what happens when Esther is read from a first-world context. Accustomed as we are to admire the "lifestyles of the rich and famous," it is hard not to admire Ahasuerus's success. We read the lavish descriptions of his court and secretly want what he has.

Yet once again, this reaction may not be what the author hopes to elicit. While there may well be a certain level of aesthetic appreciation for the luxuries described, the Bible is uniformly cautious about wealth and power without moral discernment. The psalmist pleads, for instance, "Turn my heart to your decrees, and not to selfish gain. Turn my eyes from looking at vanities; give me life in your ways" (Ps. 119:36–37). Joyce Baldwin observes that "Jewish listeners, brought up on the Prophets, were sure to be making their own observations, and silently assessing the injustice of a system that created so great a gulf

26

between rich and poor" (55). Levenson, as well, points out that this narrative is

> so focused on the external trappings that it leaves the perspicacious reader wondering what the internal life of Ahasuerus can be like. On this, there is not a word, but contextualized within the moral universe of the Hebrew Bible, especially its wisdom literature, this enormous emphasis on wealth and status cannot speak well for the man who holds the world's most powerful office. (45)

In short, those of us who preach and teach this text cannot take for granted that our listeners will understand the irony and the critique that are embedded in its telling. If the first step is to call attention to the author's comic tone, then the second is to make it clear that humor can also convey some very serious points.

Chapter 1 ends with the king rushing to reach the post office before it closes. Within the space of a few verses the high and mighty Ahasuerus has been defied, manipulated, and roundly humiliated. While this much is obvious to his advisors, his citizens, and now to us, the readers, Ahasuerus seems largely out of touch with reality. It is a characteristic that will surface again and again in subsequent chapters.

PART TWO

ESTHER 2

Esther 2:1–4

The Morning After

The mood is much changed at the beginning of chapter 2. Gone are the lawyers and the secretaries, the caterers and the guests, the pomp and the circumstance. Gone, too, is Ahasuerus's anger. We are not told exactly how long it has taken him to cool down (the opening phrase "after these things" is imprecise), but the scene has all the symptoms of the "morning after." For a brief moment, we see Ahasuerus as a man and not a king. He is lonely and depressed, contemplating a decision that has left a very poor taste in his mouth.

The phrase "he remembered Vashti and what she had done" is wonderfully ambiguous. While the most obvious antecedent is her act of defiance, the fact that this is not specified leaves room for the possibility of other more wistful memories. Perhaps she had not been such a bad wife after all.

One notices, as well, that he remembers her fate in a passive light. The characterization "what had been decreed against her" distances him from direct responsibility. While this may reflect Ahasuerus's own rationalizations, it also has the effect of underscoring his tendency to allow others to manipulate him.

We soon see that not much has changed in this regard. Verse 2 finds Ahasuerus surrounded by the royal valets, eager to cheer him up with a plan. Their proposal is anything but modest, but in that regard is consistent with the pattern of excess we have come to expect in his court. They suggest that "beautiful young virgins" (more about that phrase in a moment) be rounded up throughout all the provinces of the kingdom and brought into the safekeeping of the king's eunuch, Hegai. After the women receive their requisite beauty treatments, the king can select Vashti's replacement.

Like Athena springing full-grown from the head of Zeus, this plan seems to have been gestating in the servants' minds and now emerges fully formed. Ahasuerus does not have to worry about any of the details;

they have already been worked out in advance by these helpful servants. They do not even bother with the standard "If it pleases the king" preface (see 1:19; 3:9; 5:4, 8; 7:3; 8:5; and 9:3). Again, the reader is left wondering whether the high and mighty Ahasuerus ever makes a decision that hasn't been prompted by someone else. It is a question that will come up again and again as the story unfolds.

It may not be insignificant that the word used to describe these servants is "young men" (*naʿărîm*). Many commentators have noted the contrast between them and the "officials" (*śārîm*) of chapter 1. In any case, their concern for the king seems more personal than political. Their proposal certainly takes psychology into account. Not just young women should be sought, but virgins, and good-looking ones at that. (The four Hebrew words used to fashion this appealing picture unfold like time-lapse photography.) The suggestion of special commissioners appeals to the royal penchant for bureaucracy and gives the whole plan an "official" air. The phrasing of verse 3 also puts the highest priority on security. Once gathered, the "beautiful young virgins" (note the repetition) are to be sequestered in the safekeeping of the eunuch, Hegai. No one will have access to these women but the king, since they will be triply secure—in "the citadel of Susa," in "the harem," and in the custody of a man who has no capacity to take advantage of them. The implication is that they will be for Ahasuerus's eyes only. Finally, the servants make reference to the women's beauty treatments. The Hebrew word for this is "rubbings," which is probably a reference to a beauty regimen involving massage with perfumed oils. (The noun actually comes from a verb meaning "to scour" or "to polish.")

Having effectively captured Ahasuerus's attention, the servants finish with a flourish. Literally, verse 4 reads, "Let the young woman who is pleasing in the eyes of the king be queen instead of Vashti." Not surprisingly, the plan *is* pleasing in the eyes of the king, and he acts—again—without a moment's hesitation. (Note how both the semantics and the situation echo the end of chapter 1.) The servants' proposal seems to have been a smashing success. In the space of a few sentences, Ahasuerus has been restored to his royal self.

Esther 2:5–11
Esther Is Caught in the Royal Dragnet

The scene shifts abruptly in verse 5, as the narrative takes us beyond the walls of the palace and into the lives of two obscure Jews:

Mordecai and his cousin/adopted daughter, Esther. The transition may not be as abrupt as it seems, however. Certain conceptual bridges connect the two scenes. One is struck, for instance, by the references to Esther and Mordecai's ancestors being carried into exile. (This is especially hard to miss in the Hebrew, which uses variations on the root "remove" [gālāh] four times in the space of one verse.) Having just heard about the king's plan to carry off all the beautiful young virgins in the land, we immediately make the connection between the two groups of captives. The fact that they are "removed" from their homes and families sets up the possibility that Esther may soon be doubly exiled. As Jon Levenson points out, the personal mirrors the political (54–56).

The narrator takes a good bit of trouble to establish Esther and Mordecai's family tree, tracing their lineage back several generations along the branch of Benjamin. Commentators have long been confused about the details of this genealogy. One way of reading the Hebrew would seem to imply that Mordecai himself had been carried off into exile, which would make him well over 100 years old at the time of this story (estimates range from 114 to 120). Another way of reading the Hebrew interprets Mordecai's great-grandfather, Kish, as the one who was carried off, which clearly makes better sense historically. As we noted in chapter 1, however, precise historical accuracy may not have been foremost in this author's mind. In either case, the author does seem to be making an effort to establish a connection between Mordecai and the house of Saul. (King Saul was, remember, a Benjaminite whose father's name was Kish; see 1 Sam. 9:1–2.) The relevance of this connection will become clear as the rivalry between Mordecai and Haman the Agagite develops, since it reflects an ancient rivalry between Saul and Agag (see 1 Sam. 15). More will be said about the significance of this rivalry in our discussion of chapter 3. For now, it is enough to note its ominous presence.

Another proleptic detail may be in the names of the main characters themselves. Both the names "Esther" and "Mordecai" sound suspiciously like the names of the Babylonian deities, "Ishtar" and "Marduk." Esther's Hebrew name, Hadassah (meaning "myrtle"), is highlighted as well, however. It is almost as if a double identity is set up for her from the first. She is both grand gentile goddess and humble Hebrew flower. Similarly, Mordecai maintains a double identity throughout the book. While he has no Hebrew name per se, he is consistently identified as a "Jew." (In Hebrew the term is "Judahite," but after the exile this name was used indiscriminately for all Hebrews, and not just those from the tribe of Judah.) Thus, the book's two main characters maintain a dual identity. Each will deal with the requisite difficulties in his or her own way, but the tensions and dangers they experience are equally real. Their struggle to live faithfully within these tensions reflects the plight of their people, and hints at one of the most powerful themes in the book (see Introduction, pp. 10–14).

The parallel between Esther and the exiles is nowhere more apparent than in verse 8. She, too, is taken captive. The fact that the relevant verbs ("were gathered" and "was taken") are in the passive is crucial. Neither the virgins nor the Jews had much say in the matter of their captivity. This is particularly important for interpreting the subsequent verses. Just because Esther makes the best of a bad situation does not mean it is anything other than a bad situation. One is reminded of Jeremiah's letter to the exiles, advising them to

> build houses and live in them; plant gardens and eat what they produce. Take wives and have sons and daughters; take wives for your sons, and give your daughters in marriage, that they may bear sons and daughters; multiply there, and do not decrease. But seek the welfare of the city where I have sent you into exile, and pray to the LORD on its behalf, for in its welfare you will find your welfare. (Jer. 29:5–7)

Modern readers may be tempted to view this scene as an "innocent" beauty contest. Yet this modern association is highly misleading. For one thing, contestants in modern beauty contests choose to participate. For another, they get to go home when it is over (some with scholarships and parting gifts). But there are no parting gifts for the women caught in Ahasuerus's dragnet, and they do not get to go home. They go straight into the king's harem. However luxurious their accommodations (and one wonders if our notion of harem life has been influenced by Hollywood), it is still a poor substitute for freedom, home, and family.

Another consideration that must certainly loom large for Esther is the prospect of living in a gentile court as the concubine of a gentile king. She faces the prospect of being doubly violated, both as a woman and a Jew. That she obeys her cousin Mordecai's command in concealing her Hebrew identity does nothing to diminish this sense of violation. In fact, it intensifies it, since obeying must have been the cause of much moral discomfort. In a sense, she is being asked to relinquish the last obvious vestiges of her former identity. The fact that Mordecai gives her these orders at all must indicate that he thinks her Jewishness puts her at some risk. Small wonder he paces daily in front of the court of the harem, straining for word of how she is doing. In a sense he is pacing between pride and despair—gratified by her success, yet anxious for her safety.

In sum, these verses tell us a great deal about the character of both Esther and Mordecai. Mordecai emerges as a loyal Jew and a

31

responsible father figure. Esther, in the words of one writer, is "more than just a pretty face." Her worth is quickly recognized not only by the readers, but also by the eunuch, Hegai, who grants her special favors and "promotes" her to first place in the harem. Under the circumstances, one has to wonder whether she regards this as bane or blessing. As readers, this is yet another moment when we do not know whether to laugh or cry.

Esther 2:12–18

Esther Is Chosen as Queen

Twelve months is a long time to spend in the beauty parlor. Yet this is the span of time specified by the author for the candidates' "cosmetic treatments." The Hebrew word "rubbings" suggests that some form of massage was involved, first with oil of myrrh (an expensive and aromatic import), and then with other unspecified perfumes.

Some have suggested that this is another example of the excess of the Persian court, or alternately, of the author's tendency to exaggerate. Either way, the effect is to underscore the rigorous beauty regimen to which the women were subjected. Perhaps more important than the length of the process is the fact that it is described as a "law" (Hebrew *dāt*; NRSV "regulations"). This word is an important one in the book of Esther, being used to describe not only what was customary (1:8, 13), but also what was irrevocably decreed (9:13). The impression is that everything is being done "decently and in order." Esther is subject to these laws and customs and complies with them inasmuch as possible. Although it is a small thing, this instance joins with others to form a general impression of obedience to Persian law. Later, when Haman accuses the Jews of not keeping the king's laws (3:8), this example of Esther's compliance will come back to us as an argument in her and her people's defense.

The narrator continues the description of the selection process in verses 13–14. Each young woman is given one chance to impress the king. In addition to beauty and personality, each is allowed to take something with her when she leaves Hegai's harem. The lack of specificity here is tantalizing, and we immediately wonder what Esther will choose. But the narrator moves resolutely on, describing the process by which the women then "graduate" to a new status as concubines. After their one night with the king, they are transferred to a second harem under the care of another eunuch, Shaashgaz. There they will remain, unless the king has reason to remember them fondly and summons them again by name.

Even if the king does not remember Esther's name, the narrator seems determined that we will. The description of Esther's turn (vv. 15–18) begins with Esther's full name, used here for the first time: "Esther daughter of Abihail the uncle of Mordecai, who had adopted her as his own daughter." Even though this designation is weighted down with male relatives, it is, nonetheless, her name. Its use signals her emergence as a discreet character who will, from this time forward, begin to exert a certain level of independence.

As if to illustrate this, Esther immediately takes action. Granted, it is the first time she has been allowed to do so. Up until this moment, she has been a woman more acted upon than acting. Yet in this, her first opportunity to exercise her own will, she chooses wisely. When offered the chance to take whatever she wants from the harem, she asks "for nothing except what Hegai the king's eunuch, who had charge of the women, advised" (v. 15). While it may seem like something of a letdown for her to defer to someone else at this point, the decision may well represent the better part of wisdom. Who would be more familiar, after all, with the king's most intimate preferences than Hegai, the keeper of Ahasuerus's harem? That we are not let in on the secret is frustrating in the extreme, but perhaps the details are better left to the imagination. Regardless of what she brought with her, Esther's wisdom and self-control are clearly among her most important assets. As the verse concludes we cannot be sure if Ahasuerus will be impressed, but the narrator assures us that everyone else is. "Esther," he writes matter-of-factly, "was admired by all who saw her."

The ceremonial language of verse 16 hints that something highly significant is about to happen. Esther is taken (note the passive voice) to "King Ahasuerus in his royal palace in the tenth month, which is the month of Tebeth, in the seventh year of his reign." It is as if it is being inscribed in the annals even as it happens. Thus, we are hardly surprised when we are told that "the king loved Esther more than all the other women." Perhaps the only surprise is the level of tenderness that seems to be implied with words like "love," "favor," and "devotion." Lest we forget the other facets of Ahasuerus's personality, however, the author adds a potentially ominous allusion to the fate of the first queen. Verse 17 concludes with the words, "so that he set the royal crown on her head and made her queen instead of Vashti." No amount of royal language can disguise the risks inherent in that role.

As if to complete the parallel to chapter 1, verse 18 describes a "great banquet" given by the king in Esther's honor. Although its details

33

are not described to such an extent as in chapter 1, we get the impression that Ahasuerus spares no expense. All his officials and ministers are invited, a holiday (or perhaps a tax cut) is granted in the provinces, and gifts are distributed with "royal liberality." The narrator does not make much of this, but he does specify that this was all in honor of "Esther's banquet." Perhaps this is significant in the sense that Esther's introduction to the Persian people is wonderfully positive. In fact, Esther's reputation has spread like wildfire in the space of a few verses. How ironic that the queen should achieve so easily what the king cannot seem to buy for love or money.

Esther 2:19–23
God Save the King

There is an "out of the frying pan, into the fire" feel to this next section. Just when we begin to relax a bit about Esther's fate (the king has shown tenderness and generosity, Mordecai is ensconced protectively at the palace gate), we learn that a conspiracy has been spawned just outside the royal bedchamber. Two disgruntled eunuchs have made plans to "lay hands on" (i.e., assassinate) Ahasuerus. While their motive is unclear (do eunuchs need additional reasons for resentment?), their opportunity is not. As guardians of the king's private chamber, Bigthan and Teresh have easy access to the king in his most vulnerable moments. Although the narrative's focus is on the danger to Ahasuerus, Esther is at risk as well. Even if she were not present for the assassination attempt itself, her status as queen would be seriously jeopardized in the midst of a palace coup.

Before we turn to the resolution of this tension, however, there is a perplexing detail in the text that needs to be resolved. The story of the eunuchs' plot is introduced with a cryptic phrase that seems intended to clarify when the conspiracy takes place. Verse 19 begins, "When the virgins were being gathered together . . ." (The NRSV follows the Greek here.) The only gathering of virgins the reader knows about is, of course, the gathering that took place earlier in chapter 2. So our first thought is that this phrase suggests simultaneous action. That is, the following action unfolds at the same time as the king's conscription of the virgins. Yet this assumption does not bear up under closer scrutiny. Esther, as we will discover in verse 22, is already queen at the time of the conspiracy, so some other "gathering" must be implied.

The suggestion of a second gathering may explain the presence of an additional phrase in the Hebrew text, which reads, "When the virgins were being gathered together *a second time* . . ." Perhaps a helpful scribe was simply trying to make sense of the reference. Or perhaps it is a reference to a hypothetical group of virgins invited to Esther's wedding banquet. Jon Levenson, on the other hand, suggests that the similarities between 2:19–20 and 2:8–10 may point to "an instance of textual garbling" (63). Note that the story would make perfect sense if it jumped straight from verse 18 to 21.

There is really no way to resolve the question of how and why the text got this way. What we can do, however, is ask, "What is the effect of the text in its present form(s)?" Whether one reads with the Hebrew or the Greek, the reference to the gathering recalls Esther and Mordecai's "captive" status (see discussion above on vv. 5–6). Esther may be queen and Mordecai may be sitting in a position of some responsibility at the king's gate, but they are still both there under duress. The reiteration of Esther's Jewishness and Mordecai's command to keep her heritage a secret hints that Ahasuerus is not the only one in danger.

Disaster is averted, however, by what one might call a "divine coincidence." Mordecai gets wind of the conspiracy and reports it to Queen Esther. (Note that the author gives her this official title here for the first time.) Esther quickly reports the matter to the king, but is careful to give Mordecai the credit (v. 22). This detail is important not just for Esther's character (not taking credit where credit is not due), but also because Mordecai's role in the rescue will soon be forgotten. In any case, the conspirators are discovered and summarily executed. The incident is duly recorded in the royal records. At first blush, this seems to be just another example of official jargon. But as we shall see, the written record will play an important part in another rescue operation of far greater scale and significance.

PART THREE

ESTHER 3

Esther 3:1–6
Unjust Deserts

One might reasonably expect a promotion for Mordecai after his role in revealing the assassination plot. Indeed, the syntax of verse 1 (in Hebrew as well as in English) encourages us in this expectation. "After these things," it begins, and we naturally call to mind the previous chapter's dramatic conclusion. When the sentence continues with, "King Ahasuerus promoted . . . ," we feel certain we know what is coming next. Yet the syntax is a setup. Ahasuerus promotes not Mordecai, but Haman, a previously unknown character of ominous ancestry.

The significance of Haman's family tree is lost on most modern readers. Yet his pedigree is worth a moment's pause. The text identifies him as "Haman son of Hammedatha the Agagite." For those familiar with the stories of the early days of Israel's monarchy, this identification calls to mind a bitter memory. First Samuel 15 relates Saul's failure to follow orders with regard to the ritual execution of Agag, the king of the Amalekites. When the prophet Samuel discovers that Agag has been spared, he pronounces the oracle that effectively strips Saul of the kingship.

This association alone would be enough to make us suspicious of any descendant of Agag. When we are reminded of Mordecai's pedigree, however, we realize that he has particular reason for resentment. Mordecai, remember, is identified in Esther 2:5 as being a Benjaminite—that is, of the same tribe as Saul. In other words, there is every reason for "bad blood" between Haman and Mordecai on the basis of their family history alone. When Ahasuerus promotes Haman instead of Mordecai, it adds insult to injury. In a twisted echo of the lawyers' advice in 1:19, Mordecai's well-deserved seat of honor has been given to one who is *not* better than he.

This bit of background may go a long way toward explaining Mordecai's subsequent behavior in chapter 3, though the narrator never brings the background into the foreground long enough for us to be sure. What *is* clear is that the king's servants are mystified when Mordecai refuses to bow down to Haman. Verse 3 records their incredulity: "Why do you disobey the king's command?" they ask, referring to the fact that Ahasuerus had expressly commanded that all must "bow down and do obeisance" to the passing Haman (v. 2). Mordecai never explains, and we and the king's servants are left to wonder why.

Perhaps a short inventory of possible explanations is in order. As suggested previously, Mordecai's refusal may have had to do with a simmering family feud between his and Haman's ancestors. This is, after all, the only clue within the text itself as to Mordecai's motives.

Others have suggested that the explanation lies along more explicitly religious lines. Another story of captive Jews refusing to bow down comes to mind, namely, the story of Shadrach, Meshach, and Abednego in the third chapter of the book of Daniel. Yet this explanation is doubly weak. First, the text itself makes no mention of idolatry. Indeed, such an overt emphasis on religion would be out of character in this book, which goes out of its way not even to mention the name of God. Second, the words translated "bow down" and "do obeisance" do not always denote acts of worship, but simply respect. There is no prohibition against bowing down to another person. In 2 Samuel 14:4, for instance, the wise woman of Tekoa bows down and does obeisance before King David. In Ruth 2:10 Ruth falls prostrate before Boaz. So a moral stand against idolatry as an explanation for Mordecai's reluctance seems doubtful.

The only other possibility that seems even remotely plausible is that Mordecai is simply being stubborn. Maybe he, too, thought he deserved a promotion—or at least some recognition for saving the king's life—and resents the fact that Haman is getting all the glory. Perhaps he is simply having a fit of pique.

Readers who are uncomfortable with ambiguity are apt to try to resolve the mystery of Mordecai's motives with rather more certainty than the text allows. In truth, the narrator leaves us wondering. While this may frustrate us, it makes Mordecai a much more interesting character. In the end we can be sure of only two things: first, that Mordecai's attitude is uncompromising and that, second, it has serious consequences. To those consequences we now turn.

When Mordecai refuses to bow down to Haman he is, in fact, breaking the law. The servants' question in verse 3 calls attention to this. No matter what Mordecai's motives are, his refusal is an act of civil disobedience. The fact that Mordecai chooses to disobey a direct order of the king raises the stakes significantly.

After repeated attempts to convince Mordecai to comply with the king's command, the servants finally inform Haman of Mordecai's

37

behavior. (Was Haman not alert enough to notice on his own?) One gets the sense that, to the servants' credit, they were reluctant to do this. Yet their revelation may have some connection to a revelation of Mordecai's own. Verse 4 says that they tell Haman, "in order to see whether Mordecai's words would avail; for he had told them that he was a Jew." Later in the story Haman's wife and friends make a comment that may shed some light on this otherwise obscure line. "If Mordecai, before whom your downfall has begun, is of the Jewish people," they warn in 6:13, "you will not prevail against him, but will surely fall before him." While the author does not bring up this apparent rumor of the Jews' invincibility at this point in the story, it may offer some explanation for the servants' reasoning here. They seem to want to test Haman's prowess against the strength of Mordecai and his God, or perhaps, test the Jewish God's loyalty to Mordecai. In any case, this is the first time Mordecai is identified publicly as a Jew. The addition of this detail raises the stakes again as we realize that this may be more than just an individual matter.

Once the servants point out Mordecai's refusal to bow down, Haman takes note of it and is—perhaps understandably—enraged. What is harder to understand is the intensity of that rage. Thinking it "beneath him to lay hands on Mordecai alone," Haman plots "to destroy all the Jews, the people of Mordecai, throughout the whole kingdom of Ahasuerus" (v. 6).

The disproportionate scope of Haman's rage is staggering, and there is a sense in which nothing could have prepared the reader for such barbarity. Even if we had begun to be slightly nervous about guilt by association on the basis of Mordecai's public identification as a Jew, the fact that Haman now proposes genocide as a solution to one individual's lack of respect is unimaginable. Yet there are several clues, dropped like breadcrumbs along the path of the previous narrative, that serve as hints of horrors to come. Disproportion, remember, was characteristic of the Persian court in chapters 1 and 2. Ahasuerus's lavish banquets strained credulity in both length and opulence. The king's reaction to both the disobedient Vashti and the search for her successor seemed unnecessarily "over the top." Then there was the matter of the apparently unjust promotion of Haman on the heels of Mordecai's act of loyalty. Throughout the book there has been a pattern of people getting far less—or more—than they deserve. Excess, disproportion, and overreaction seem to be the order of the day in Ahasuerus's court. What we realize now, however, is that we "haven't seen anything yet." Haman makes Ahasuerus look like Mr. Moderation.

The text itself encourages us to make such comparisons. The last time we heard the word "rage" (*ḥēmāh*) was in 1:12, when Vashti

38

refused to come when called and "the king was enraged, and his anger burned within him." This was the passion that first threw things out of balance and set the present story in motion. There is also the matter of a not-so-subtle play on words in 3:5. Literally, the last phrase of this verse reads, "Haman was filled with *ḥēmāh*." Even Haman's name is full of sound and fury. We realize all this in retrospect, however, and the readers are caught unaware along with "all the Jews, the people of Mordecai, throughout the whole kingdom of Ahasuerus" (v. 6). The phrases are as relentlessly thorough as Haman himself.

Esther 3:7–11
Haman's Lucky Day

For all his fury, Haman is still a highly methodical man. (Perhaps this is precisely what makes him so dangerous.) In an act of hideous irony, Haman calls together his unnamed prognosticators to determine "an auspicious day for mass murder" (Levenson, 2; cf. 70 and Paton, 201). Note that he does not first look for a lucky day to make his immodest proposal to the king. No, he is so confident of his success in that regard that the "lot" (*pūr*) is cast to set the day for the genocide itself. This being settled, he can proceed to put his plan before Ahasuerus, confident that everything has been done decently and in order.

A brief aside might be helpful with regard to the casting of lots. Although the foreign sailors in the book of Jonah also engage in this practice as a way of determining the will of the gods (Jonah 1:7), the practice was common in Israel as well (see Num. 26:55–56 for one of many examples). It is almost certainly the Akkadian word for lot, *pūrū*, that gives the Hebrew festival associated with the book of Esther, Purim, its name. The irony of its use in the present passage is compounded, however, when we realize that it may be Mordecai's God rather than Haman's gods who determine the "lucky" day. After all, the date is set a full twelve months in the future, thus giving the Jews time to prepare and the plot of the story time to unfold. Perhaps this stroke of providence is a preview of the help "from another quarter" that Mordecai refers to in 4:14. In any case, the date turns out to be far more propitious for the Jews than it is for Haman.

Haman's argument before Ahasuerus is a triumph of misconstrual and manipulation. From the first his words are calculated to disconcert. "A certain people," he points out, are "scattered and separated

39

among the peoples in all the provinces of your kingdom" (v. 8). On the face of it, this would not seem especially damning. The next bit of information (or misinformation) makes it so, however. "Their laws are different from those of every other people, and they do not keep the king's laws," Haman asserts. Now the fact that this unnamed people is "scattered" seems to imply that they have in fact infiltrated the entire kingdom. That they are "separated" hints that they hold themselves aloof from the Persians, perhaps thinking themselves superior to their masters, refusing to assimilate to local custom or submit to political accountabilities.

How dare they! we may expect the king to stammer. Yet, either because Haman cannot wait to rush on with his murderous plan or because he does not trust Ahasuerus to get the point, Haman helps the king to a conclusion by saying, "so that it is not appropriate for the king to tolerate them." Sensing, perhaps, that he may have overstepped, he then prefaces his proposal with the obligatory "If it pleases the king . . ." (v. 9). What follows, however, is what will please Haman, and the degree to which he wants it is indicated by his offer to pay for the pogrom out of his own pocket. "Let a decree be issued for their destruction," he proposes, "and I will pay ten thousand talents of silver into the hands of those who have charge of the king's business, so that they may put it into the king's treasuries."

If the king were to balk at the wholesale destruction of so many of his subjects, the fabulous bribe is calculated to distract if not silence his objections. Scholars disagree as to the exact amount of Haman's offer, quibbling over whether one court official could actually have come up with the cash equivalent of two-thirds of Persia's annual gross national product (see Moore and Paton). What no one seems to have considered, however, is that Haman could be bluffing. Ahasuerus apparently turns down the bribe ("the money is given to you," v. 11, though some maintain that this simply indicates Ahasuerus's permission to use the money in whatever way Haman sees fit), so it does not really matter whether Haman has that much money or not. One thing is indisputably evident, however. The possibly exaggerated and certainly extravagant sum is an index of just how much Haman hates Mordecai—and by extension—all the Jews.

At this point, we wait along with Haman for the king's decision. Also along with Haman, we know more than King Ahasuerus does. Haman, remember, has left out several significant "details," not the least of which is a description of the incident that inspired his indignation. We might reasonably hope that a wise king would make some inquiries about the situation and thus discover the unfortunate "spin" that

40

Haman has placed on the facts. If Ahasuerus had bothered to inquire, he would certainly have discovered that the punishment was wildly out of proportion to the crime. But Ahasuerus does not inquire. Just as we saw him do in chapter 1 with regard to Vashti, and in chapter 2 with regard to the search for her replacement, the ever-suggestible Ahasuerus takes the advice of his courtiers after hardly a moment's pause for consideration. Sympathetic readers and Haman must now part company in perspective as—to our horror and Haman's delight—the king removes his signet ring and hands it over to Haman (v. 10). This act gives Haman the power to do as he pleases, and with the king's imprimatur. Lest we miss the magnitude of this act, the narrator hammers it home by reminding us of Haman's unambiguously ominous credentials: ". . . gave it to Haman son of Hammedatha the Agagite, the enemy of the Jews."

As the section ends in verse 11, Haman has his hands full, both literally and figuratively. He has the king's own signet ring, of course. But he also has the money (whether his or Ahasuerus's) to carry out his plan. Finally, in a terrifying flourish, Ahasuerus places the people themselves in Haman's hands, telling him to "do with them as it seems good to you." From Haman's perspective, he has it all.

Esther 3:12–14
Signed, Sealed, and Delivered

With speed and efficiency to rival modern express mail, the edict is transcribed, translated, and sent out "to every province in its own script and every people in its own language" (v. 12). This description echoes chapter 1 exactly. There, remember, the decree attempted to dictate that all men should be master in their own house (1:22). But while the first decree was tinged with comic irony, this one is deadly serious. The only hint of irony is tragic irony, in that the edict is issued on "the thirteenth day of the first month"—that is, the day before Passover (Levenson, 73; cf. Exod. 12:6 and Lev. 23:5). Although the text does nothing to underscore that irony, the mere mention of the date is enough to suggest a connection. For all intents and purposes, it looks as if the order for the Jews' destruction has been issued on the eve of the anniversary of their greatest deliverance. Whether the juxtaposition inspires bitterness or hope is impossible to say.

The irrevocability of the edict is emphasized with the words, "it was written in the name of King Ahasuerus and sealed with the king's ring" (v. 12). Further, all possibility of misunderstanding is preempted by the multiple translations and scripts. Finally, no province is too far-flung for the king's couriers. No one is to escape. Young and old, women and children are specified, and the attackers are given express permission to plunder. Haman is nothing if not efficient.

Yet there is a hint that he is even more sinister than we imagined. In his original proposal to the king in verse 9, Haman asked that a decree be issued for the people's "destruction" (from the verb ʾābad). If there was any doubt as to his murderous intentions, the written version of the decree prefaces "to destroy" (ʾābad) with the seemingly superfluous verbs "to kill" and "to annihilate." Is this just a case of "overkill," or is something more significant going on? (Note: For some reason the NRSV reverses the order of these three verbs in translation. This reversal does not affect the following argument.)

There is no possibility of misunderstanding Haman's intentions in the written form of the decree. But there is an important level of ambiguity in the oral version. Sandra Beth Berg points out that the words for "destroy" (ʾābad) and for "enslave" (ʿābad) are virtual homophones, that is, they sound alike, but are quite different in meaning and derivation (Berg, 101–2). An example in English would be the words "alter" and "altar." Let us go back for a moment and revisit Haman's proposal as Ahasuerus may have heard it in verses 8 and 9.

At the end of verse 8, Haman says that "it is not appropriate for the king to tolerate" the Jews. Literally, this translates, "it is not appropriate for the king to let them rest." With this in mind, how would Ahasuerus have been most likely to hear the proposal in verse 9? Berg suggests that he could well have heard, "If it please the king, let a decree be issued for their enslavement" (ʾābad vs. ʿābad). The two words sound almost exactly alike. Yet their meaning is quite different. Add to this the fact that Haman follows up the proposal with an offer of payment, and Berg's suggestion seems even more plausible. At the risk of making excuses for Ahasuerus, this could explain why he acquiesced to Haman's plan so quickly (though it hardly exonerates him, since he would still be agreeing to the enslavement of a significant portion of the population on extremely scant evidence).

Having looked back, let us now look forward. Berg's homophone theory goes a long way toward explaining Esther's words in 7:4. There, Esther explains her request for clemency by saying, "If we had been sold merely as slaves, men and women, I would have held my peace." Although there is more to be said about her words, for now let it suffice to say that the destruction/enslavement ambiguity makes sense of

42

her otherwise puzzling argument.

Part of the reason it is so important to discuss this theory in the context of chapter 3 has to do with Haman's character. While it is obvious that he is a formidable enemy for the Jews, his considerable cunning may not be so obvious. That he could stoop to this kind of rhetorical trick—and hope to get away with it—catapults him into the category of evil genius. And it leaves the readers wondering if he will ever meet his match.

Another reason to call attention to this theory is to underscore the importance and power of a written text. Ambiguity may abide at the oral level, but once words are written down, they take on a terrible finality. "Enslavement" (ʿābad) and "destruction" (ʾābad) to the ear may have left room for doubt, but when "destruction" (ʾābad) is written down, it is unambiguous. "Kill" and "annihilate" are merely nails in the coffin. This theme of the power of the written word will return at several significant junctures, and will form an important point of departure for interpretation (see Introduction, pp. 14–16).

The chapter closes with one last stroke of irony. While the couriers are carrying out their appointed rounds in every far-flung province of the empire, the decree is issued close to home as well. While Haman and the king sit down for a drink after their hard day's work, all Susa is "thrown into confusion." One shouldn't wonder.

PART FOUR

Esther 4

Esther 4:1–3
A Grief Observed

If the book of Esther were a movie, chapter 3 might end with a close-up of Haman and the king, ensconced in the comfort of the palace having a civilized drink of sherry (though given the descriptions of the king's drinking habits in chapter 1, we might better imagine boilermakers). Then the camera would pan out over the city and the clink of their glasses would be drowned out by the cries of confusion outside the palace walls.

The confusion at the end of chapter 3 is generic. Presumably, the Persians are as confused as the Jews, just in a different way. Perhaps they are perplexed—or even grieved—by Ahasuerus's order to murder so many of their neighbors. Or some may have greeted the edict with greedy anticipation, anxious for the opportunity to settle old scores and get rich in the bargain. The fact is, we are not told. The nature of the confusion at the end of chapter 3 is general and dramatic, but tantalizingly unspecific.

At the beginning of chapter 4, the focus becomes wrenchingly specific. The camera zooms in on one man: Mordecai. We see him tearing his clothes in the traditional Middle-Eastern gesture of mourning. He puts on sackcloth and ashes, and goes through the city "wailing with a loud and bitter cry" (v. 1). His wanderings culminate at the gate of the palace. There he stops and stays, though we are given the impression that he might have gone further if not for the fact that he is woefully out of compliance with the palace dress code (v. 2).

One is struck immediately by the very public nature of Mordecai's grief. He seems to want to attract as much attention as possible. This is understandable given the very human urge to unmask injustice, especially injustice on such an overwhelming scale. More will be said in a moment about some possible negative consequences of his behavior, but for now, let it suffice to say that his grief is great. More important,

44

it is in proportion to the gravity of the situation. This sets Mordecai's character in stark contrast with Haman (and to a lesser extent Ahasuerus), whose hallmark has been a consistent display of disproportion.

While Mordecai's grief is the focus of these two verses, the description is not so detailed as to probe into the specific reasons for his grief. While the main one is obvious—namely, the impending destruction of his people—we are left to wonder whether he feels any personal responsibility for their peril. Would he have acted differently had he known the consequences of refusing to bow down to Haman? To what extent was his behavior a personal issue? A moral issue? A religious issue? Does he now regret it? The text is resolutely silent about such ruminations, so interpreters must be content to leave such questions unanswered. (Part of the artistry of this book, however, is its knack for making us ask them!)

Verse 3 broadens the focus again, and we see that Mordecai's grief is but a sample of the great spasm of grief that grips the Jewish people throughout all the provinces of Persia. This is important, because not since the description of the exile in 2:5–6—a past event from the perspective of the present story—have we had such a sense that the fate of Mordecai and the fate of his people are inextricably intertwined. The identification of the one with the other is now set. For the purposes of the story, it is as irrevocable as the fateful edict.

Esther 4:4–8

What Does the Queen Know, and When Does She Know It?

Esther, too, is "deeply distressed" by the news brought to her by her maids and eunuchs. But as we continue to read of her reaction, we realize that she has been told very little. Apparently, she has not been informed of the edict at all. Rather, her distress is due to the fact that Mordecai is sitting at the king's gate in sackcloth and ashes. It is only when he refuses the garments that she sends that Haʾhach, the king's eunuch, is dispatched to "go to Mordecai to learn what was happening and why" (v. 5).

These two verses are wonderfully revealing. First, they call our attention to the contrast between life inside the palace and outside the palace. We got an important glimpse of this at the end of chapter 3 when

45

Haman and Ahasuerus sat down for a drink while all Susa was thrown into a panic. But these verses highlight how isolated the palace really is. Information is tightly controlled, presumably by Haman. (He was, after all, the one who "broke the news" to Ahasuerus in chapter 3 about the dangerous and disobedient people within the kingdom's borders.) So in spite of the fact that the edict's content is being proclaimed far and wide by the king's state-of-the-art courier service, the news has not spread within the palace walls themselves.

The second thing these verses reveal is Esther's growing sense of personal danger. What is the nature of her distress, after all, at the beginning of verse 4? Her maids and eunuchs evidently know about her association with Mordecai or they would not have thought to bring her the news about his inappropriate presence at the king's gate. So her distress seems to be centered in the need to keep their relationship—and her Jewishness—a secret. Mordecai, remember, had "charged her not to tell" when she was first taken into the harem (2:10). Although she does not know it yet, the risks of guilt by association are astronomically greater than when he originally gave that order. If her personal servants know of the relationship, then how many more people might know, especially if Mordecai keeps calling attention to himself at the gate? Part of her distress must surely stem from confusion over Mordecai's "mixed signals." First he tells her to keep quiet about her Jewishness, and then he seems determined to call everyone's attention to it!

At Esther's behest, Hathach seeks out Mordecai "in the open square of the city in front of the king's gate" (v. 6). In this very public venue, Mordecai tells Hathach "all that had happened to him" (v. 7a). This is a curious phrase, and at first it seems a bit self-centered. Its position at the beginning of a sequence, however, suggests that Mordecai is telling the story from the very beginning, namely, with his refusal to bow before Haman. It is interesting, though, that he describes this as something that has "happened" to him or "befallen him." In Mordecai's mind, then, he seems to have had little choice in the matter and thus bears little responsibility. This phrase may clarify some of the questions raised above about the nature of his grief (re vv. 1–2).

Mordecai continues by telling Hathach "the exact sum of money that Haman had promised to pay into the king's treasuries for the destruction of the Jews" (v. 7b). How does Mordecai know this? The conversation between Haman and Ahasuerus took place within the palace, after all (3:7–11). Evidently information leaks out of the palace better than it leaks in. This phrase is significant not only because it reveals that Mordecai knows how much it is worth to Haman to destroy the Jews, but because it reveals that Mordecai is well connected. Perhaps this should not surprise us, since Mordecai was the one who got wind of the assassination attempt in time to alert the king (2:21–23). One can learn a lot, it seems, by keeping one's ear to the ground at the palace gate.

Finally, Mordecai produces an actual "copy of the written decree issued in Susa for their destruction" (v. 8a). In light of our earlier discussion about the possible oral ambiguities of the word for "destruction" (ʾābad), this written copy is crucial. If Mordecai had simply communicated the content of the decree orally, there would be a possibility that Esther would think that enslavement (ʿābad) was the "only" thing at issue. With the written copy, however, Haman's intent is murderously clear.

Mordecai's intentions are clear as well. He gives Hathach the copy "that he might show it to Esther, explain it to her, and charge her to go to the king to make supplication to him and entreat him for her people" (v. 8). No more mixed messages from Mordecai, then. In issuing this charge, he effectively countermands his own previous orders about keeping her identity a secret. Esther is to abandon all attempts at anonymity and plead for "her people." In Mordecai's mind, then, her fate is as inextricably intertwined with the Jews as his own.

Esther 4:9–17
God Save the Queen

This is not yet clear in Esther's mind, however.

Hathach relays Mordecai's message (v. 9), but Esther responds with one of her own (vv. 10–11). Has Mordecai forgotten, she asks, that the punishment for approaching the king in the inner court without an invitation is death? "Only if the king holds out the golden scepter to someone," she patiently explains both to Mordecai and to us, "may that person live." She then adds a bit of ominous information that even Mordecai and his well-placed sources could not have known: "I myself have not been called to come in to the king for thirty days." Has the king's ardor cooled, then, making her welcome even more uncertain?

Commentators have not always been kind to Esther concerning these verses. Her hesitation has sometimes been construed as cowardice and/or selfishness. Yet one can hardly blame her for being cautious. The fate of her predecessor, Vashti, must have loomed large in her mind (Levenson, 80). Her comments also indicate how clearly she is thinking (no small feat under the circumstances), and how much she

47

has learned about the customs of the Persian court. Most important, Esther's words reflect the ways in which her character has developed since we saw her last. (This versus those who see the characters in this book as only "type" characters that remain static throughout the story.) She has learned to think and act for herself, and is no longer content to take orders from Mordecai without carefully considering their wisdom first. The one thing that Mordecai and Vashti have in common as characters, after all, is their propensity for headstrong and precipitous action. Esther's deliberate approach to problems—both now and later—sets her apart from both of them.

Commentators have also puzzled over the rigidity of the court rules Esther describes in this verse. The Greek historian, Herodotus, too, tells of the prohibition of entering the Persian throne room uninvited, but notes that one could send a message requesting an audience (see esp. 1:99 and 3:118; cf. Levenson, 80). Could not Esther have requested such an audience? After all, she had a year before the edict was to take effect.

Such questions fail to remain within the framework of the story itself. If, as we maintained in the Introduction (pp. 4–5), the book of Esther is best classified as "historical fiction" (or more specifically as "burlesque"), then the author is allowed a certain literary license by virtue of the genre. Questions such as these hold the book to an unfair standard of historical accuracy and introduce issues that are foreign to the story itself. For this author's purposes, the "rules of the game" are the ones that Esther describes in this verse. A much fairer question to put to the narrative would be, "How do these "rules affect the story?" For one thing, they choreograph the plot in two subsequent chapters (5 and 8). But further, they focus all our attention on one highly dramatic moment. The whole story hinges on whether or not Ahasuerus will extend that golden scepter. It may be murky history, but it is mesmerizing drama.

Hathach shuttles back with Mordecai's reply (though the plural "they" in verse 12 suggests that there may have been more than one go-between). Mordecai's response is important enough to quote verses 13 and 14 in their entirety:

> Do not think that in the king's palace you will escape any more than all the other Jews. For if you keep silence at such a time as this, relief and deliverance will rise for the Jews from another quarter, but you and your father's family will perish. Who knows? Perhaps you have come to royal dignity for just such a time as this.

Whether or not such a conclusion is warranted, Mordecai seems to have interpreted Esther's hesitancy as—guess what—cowardice and/or selfishness. His opening words in verse 13 are a pointed reminder that she can die now or she can die later, but her life is in jeopardy either way. Her only chance—from a purely personal standpoint—is to risk approaching the king.

Mordecai's logic is flawless. Yet his assumptions may be inaccurate. Esther, remember, has been under orders from Mordecai himself to keep her identity a secret. Although he is evidently countermanding those orders (v. 8), she may not be convinced that this is her—or the Jews'—best option. If she does not reveal her Jewishness, then she could well escape by keeping silent. And perhaps there might be a less reckless plan for everyone concerned. From Esther's perspective, then, Mordecai's statement, "Do not think that in the king's palace you will escape any more than all the other Jews," must have seemed like a thinly veiled threat. If she does not reveal her identity, he will!

We can never be sure, of course, that Mordecai intended his words in this way, but it is important to understand that there may be a sense in which the two characters are "talking past each other" in this passage. In any event, he tries another tack in verse 14. Assuming that Esther is considering silence as a means of saving herself and abandoning her people, Mordecai suggests that she may not be the only means of deliverance. What exactly he has in mind with regard to this "relief and deliverance" that may "rise for the Jews from another quarter" is unclear. In any case, it is the closest thing in the entire book to an overt reference to God's presence and power to intervene in the interest of a happy ending (cf. Introduction, pp. 13–14).

After working the providence angle in a negative way, Mordecai now puts a more positive spin on it. "Who knows?" he speculates. Perhaps Esther has "come to royal dignity for just such a time as this."

Of all Mordecai's arguments, this one is at once the most powerful and the most personal. Here we glimpse again the worried guardian, pacing back and forth in front of the harem, worried about the fate of the young woman he has raised as his own (2:11). There is a sense in which these words summarize and attempt to make sense of all that has happened to Esther so far. They acknowledge in one breath all her pain and all her possibilities.

We cannot be sure which—if any—of Mordecai's arguments wins Esther over. We only know that she agrees to go along with Mordecai's plan. Verse 16 reads:

> Go, gather all the Jews to be found in Susa, and hold a fast on my behalf, and neither eat nor drink for three days, night or day. I and my maids will also fast as you do. After that I will go to the king, though it is against the law; and if I perish, I perish.

49

Her reply is revealing in several ways. First, it is saturated with humility and piety. She does not assume that she is going to accomplish the mission single-handedly. (Contrast this with Haman in 3:7, who is so confident he goes ahead and sets the date for the Jews' destruction even before he asks Ahasuerus.) Her reference to fasting acknowledges that she is relying on others—and perhaps God, though the reference is oblique—for success. Second, her words demonstrate uncommon bravery. If there was any question about her courage before, surely her terse "if I perish, I perish" puts such questions to rest. Third, she has completely identified with the Jewish people. The fate of the Jews is now as much hers as Mordecai's. Finally, she shows the resolution and self-possession of a true queen. Verse 16 reads like a battle plan, and she is clearly the general. Indeed, Mordecai seems to recognize this role reversal first of all. Verse 17 attests to this with its laconic conclusion: "Mordecai then went away and did everything as Esther had ordered him."

PART FIVE

ESTHER 5

Esther 5:1–8
Dinner for Three

Esther takes the initiative now, and Mordecai fades temporarily into the background. From this time forward, she is every inch a queen. Her actions and demeanor are an eloquent testimony to this. Yet the narrator helps to nudge us into a new level of recognition by referring to her for the first time as "Queen Esther" (v. 2).

Esther dons her royal dignity right along with the royal robes (v. 1; cf. 4:14). Her "uniform" stands in stark contrast to the sackcloth and ashes in which her people are dressed (4:1–3). Yet we should not be seduced by outward appearances of luxury. There are two levels of reality in this scene: inner and outer. The inner level is signaled by the phrase "the third day," which refers, of course, to the fast that Esther instituted at the end of chapter 4. For three days and nights she and her maids—along with all the Jews in Susa—have gone without food or water. Thus, her inner reality aligns her much more strongly with their weakness than her outer reality aligns her with the opulence and power of the court. As readers, we ought not to lose sight of this dangerous disparity in Esther's situation. Dressing up to visit the king uninvited is a bit like venturing into a snake pit doing one's best imitation of a snake.

Considerable attention is given to choreography in this verse. At first, this may seem like an excuse for more "royal-ese." Indeed, the stilted formality of the prose is reminiscent of the banquet description in chapter 1. But in the midst of the "royal this" and "royal that" (there are actually six words in this one verse that are cognates of the root for "king"), the author sets up an important description of the scene's layout. The throne room opens onto an inner court. When Esther comes into this court, she positions herself so as to catch Ahasuerus's eye. It is essential that we be able to picture this if we are to appreciate the ensuing scene.

One could easily imagine this scene unfolding in a much less fortunate way. Three things help it to end happily. First, Ahasuerus is

51

seated on the throne when Esther enters the court. If he hadn't been, she might have been thrown out or arrested forthwith. Second, she manages to catch his eye. This, too, is a happy stroke of providence, though Esther may deserve some of the credit in that she has taken pains with both her appearance and her position. Finally, we should also recognize a certain degree of savvy in her decision to stand in the court rather than barging directly into the throne room. While it's true that even the court was off limits, her hesitation may at least give Ahasuerus the illusion that it is his idea to invite her in.

The dramatic tension peaks in verse 2, but mercifully dissipates within the space of a few phrases. (Contrast this with the Apocrypha's prolonged and melodramatic version of this scene; see Appendix, pp. 94–95.) The moment Queen Esther catches Ahasuerus's eye, he extends the golden scepter, signaling that she has won his favor and that it is safe to approach. She obliges and touches the top of the scepter as a sign of gratitude and respect. (Readers who suspect a bit of innuendo in this verse are probably not imagining it; see Beal, 70–71.)

The extent of Ahasuerus's largesse is revealed by his offer in verse 3. "What is it, Queen Esther?" he asks. "What is your request? It shall be given you, even to the half of my kingdom." It is difficult to know whether this offer is literal or figurative, but either way, it is typically extravagant.

As readers, our relief is palpable. After the tension of Esther's entrance, this offer, coming as it does on the heels of her reprieve, is dizzying in its effect. *Ask him!* we urge her. *Plead for your people now while he's in a generous mood! This is better than anyone could have hoped!*

We are puzzled and perhaps a bit disappointed, then, when we read Esther's response in verse 4. "If it pleases the king," she begins humbly, "let the king and Haman come today to a banquet that I have prepared for the king."

Banquet? Who said anything about a banquet? Why are you wasting an opportunity like this on a dinner invitation?

Esther is more patient—and perhaps more wise—than we are, however. Notice, first, how she words the invitation. It is clearly an invitation to the king; Haman's inclusion is made to look like an afterthought. This is even more obvious in Hebrew. Literally, her invitation reads, "Let the king come—and Haman—today to the banquet that I have prepared for him" (note that "him" is singular). The care with which this invitation is crafted reveals that Esther is very much aware of the need to flatter and the risk of giving offense. It must not seem as if she views Haman and the king as being on the same level.

52

Why throw a banquet at all? The author gives us no hints as to Esther's reasoning here, but we might guess that she wants to set up a situation in which she has a stronger advantage. She has only just survived her uninvited entrance, after all. Maybe she wants to consolidate her position and give Ahasuerus more time to remember what a wonderful wife she is (not to mention the old "the way to a man's heart is through his stomach" strategy).

Now to the question of why she decides on a dinner for three. Again, we are left to guess. Perhaps it occurs to Esther that the king would have a rather different set of expectations of a dinner for two. While seduction might have worked, it is not the method that Esther chooses.

Another thing that Haman's presence makes possible is an immediate confrontation. If Esther had made her case in the throne room or at a private dinner with Ahasuerus, there would have been a gap between the moment of her accusation and the resulting confrontation with Haman. There could have been no way of guaranteeing her presence at this meeting, and thus no opportunity to press her advantage. This way, she can catch Haman off guard, giving him no time to concoct an excuse or to wriggle out of it later when it's "just between us guys." While we cannot know whether Esther anticipated such advantages, they are undeniably present, and they lead us to suspect that Haman's inclusion was anything *but* an afterthought. And they are consistent with Esther's emerging character as a careful and brilliant strategist. (Our first hint of this was the last time she was given the opportunity to make a request, namely in 2:15, when she "asked for nothing but what Hegai the king's eunuch . . . advised.")

Whatever her strategy, the king is apparently delighted with the invitation and summons Haman to the banquet with all possible speed (v. 5). Verse 6 finds the characters already at the festivities and the author wastes little time with description. The only detail that is allowed to slip through is beautifully deliberate: The king reiterates his question *while they are drinking wine.* The implication seems to be that he has eaten his fill and is now in a mellow and amenable mood. Esther has him right where she wants him.

The king's question is almost exactly as it was before, including the all-important offer to give her up to half his kingdom. Surely, now is the moment for Esther to make her appeal.

Esther prefaces her response with several preliminary phrases: "This is my petition and request: If I have won the king's favor, and if it pleases the king to grant my petition and fulfill my request . . ." (vv. 7–8a). *Is she simply being polite*, we wonder, *or is she stalling?*

53

Either way, tension mounts with each additional word. Finally, she makes her request: " . . . let the king and Haman come tomorrow to the banquet that I will prepare for them, and then I will do as the king has said" (v. 8b).

As readers, we are as mystified as Ahasuerus is at this point . . . perhaps more so, because we know what is at stake. *Why request another banquet?*

There is always the possibility that Esther has lost her nerve, in which case her delay reflects a temporary crisis of confidence. We could hardly blame her. Yet there may be other explanations that are more consistent with her character. Perhaps she senses that the moment is *not*, in fact, just right. Or perhaps she is using this moment to reframe the way her request will be received. Notice, for instance, the way the end of her response is phrased: "then I will do as the king has said." Suddenly she has made it seem as if she is doing *his* bidding instead of the other way around! In the words of one insightful reader, "Esther plays the king like a trout on a line." (Compare this scene with Abigail's masterful handling of David in 1 Sam. 25.)

Some have suggested that the author may have reasons that Esther knows not of. For instance, the delay makes the story comply with the common pattern of "three"—that is, not the first time, nor the second, but the third (as in "The Three Little Pigs"). And the delay does make it possible to set up the following scene where Haman constructs the incriminating gallows/stake on which he will eventually be executed. Yet good authors do not usually manipulate their characters in such an arbitrary way. The character has a reason for her actions, even if we cannot know for sure what it is. In this case, let's just say it works out well for both the author and for Esther.

And then there is the possibility that God is leading her to delay. Although this seems to leave the literary level behind in favor of an historical one, this is not necessarily the case. God *is* a character in this story, albeit a notoriously elusive one (see Introduction, pp. 13–14). The "ellipses" in the author's telling of the tale allow us to consider the possibility that God inspires Esther's delay in order to give Haman more rope with which to hang himself.

Esther 5:9–14

54   *Haman Develops Indigestion*

Haman leaves the banquet "happy and in good spirits" (v. 9). But his elation is short-lived. Mordecai is in his accustomed spot at the king's gate and, true to form, refuses either to rise or tremble before Haman. Levenson points out that this is actually an escalation of Mordecai's civil disobedience in that previously, he had simply refused to bow (3:2–5; Levenson, 92).

In an uncharacteristic display of self-control, Haman restrains himself and goes home (v. 10a). There, he holds what can only be called a "pity party" in which he regales his wife and friends first with a litany of his achievements and then with the grandiose conclusion that "all this does me no good so long as I see the Jew Mordecai sitting at the king's gate" (vv. 10b–13).

The expansive nature of Haman's ego is wonderfully illustrated by the way he enumerates his honors in front of the very people who must have been most familiar with them. The excessive nature of his obsession is illustrated by the fact that one uncooperative underling can completely outweigh these accomplishments. The balloon swells and swells and finally pops with the application of one small pin.

Everything about this scene conspires to create a ludicrous parody of the preceding one. There, a humble woman reluctantly takes on the trappings of royalty and risks her life to save others. Here, a megalomaniac who thinks he's royalty plots to destroy others (see Levenson again, 92).

Haman's fan club is quick to suggest a solution to his "problem." In a proposal that is worthy of Haman's ego in terms of its excess, they propose that he construct a "gallows" (literally "tree" or "piece of wood") some eighty feet high on which to hang Mordecai.

There are a few things to be said about this proposal. First, if a gallows roughly the height of a six-story building seems like "overkill," it obviously is. Yet, in spite of the fact that this strains credulity, it is completely consistent with the excesses described elsewhere in the book (remember the dimensions and duration of the banquet in chapter 1, for instance).

Second, the instrument of execution is probably not a "gallows," per se, but a huge pole or stake designed for purposes of impalement. This does not make its height any less incredible, but it is more consistent with both the Hebrew word used here and the way the ancient Persians are known to have disposed of their enemies. Perhaps the most important reason to recognize it as such is that impalement involves an added element of disgrace (Levenson, 93; Gerleman, 134). It is not enough, in other words, for Haman merely to kill Mordecai; he must disgrace him as well.

Notice, too, that Haman's wife and friends suggest that he build the structure first and then "tell the king to have Mordecai hanged on it" (v. 14). So much for painfully polite requests. Either these people

55

are very familiar with Haman's tendency to think more highly of himself than he ought to think, or they share in his presumption and overconfidence.

The real irony here is that Mordecai is already a condemned man. All Haman has to do is wait for the edict to take effect, and Mordecai (along with all the rest of the Jews) will be out of his hair forever. But patience is not one of Haman's virtues (if indeed he has any). A year, evidently, is too long to wait when one's ego is being assailed. Only a special public humiliation on an accelerated schedule will do.

Not surprisingly, Haman loves the idea. In language reminiscent of scenes where Ahasuerus laps up the suggestions of his advisors, Haman is "pleased" by this advice and has the gallows made (v. 14). Having thus taken steps to eliminate his rival, he is ready, in the words of his friends, to "go with the king to the banquet in good spirits." Yes indeed. There's nothing like anticipating a good impalement to whet one's appetite . . . (compare 3:15).

PART SIX

ESTHER 6

Esther 6:1–5
No Rest for the Wicked

Author Frederick Buechner once said that a coincidence is just God's way of remaining anonymous. If that is so, then God seems to be taking a very active—albeit low-profile—role in this chapter.

On what could well be the last night of Mordecai's life, Ahasuerus has a sudden attack of insomnia (v. 1). This is the first major "coincidence" of this scene, and the second is like unto it in significance. The king calls for the royal records to be read, obviously hoping that they will have a soporific effect. But history proves much more exciting than he expects. Of all the passages in the court records, the servant just happens to turn to the story of how Mordecai saved the king's life (v. 2; cf. 3:21–23; note that Bigthan's name is spelled differently in 6:2, but it is clearly the same person). It is all there in glorious detail; even the names of the would-be assassins are duly recorded. This is hardly the kind of bedtime reading that is likely to lull the king to sleep. Now wide awake, he asks, "What honor or distinction has been bestowed on Mordecai for this?" And the servants bluntly reply, "Nothing has been done for him" (v. 3).

In order to appreciate the importance of these two coincidences, one only has to consider how the story might have unfolded without them. Perhaps it would help to backtrack for a moment.

At the end of the previous chapter, we know that Esther is planning another banquet for the following day. We hope that this will be the occasion at which she wins a reprieve for her people. Yet we also know that Haman has put Mordecai's execution on an accelerated schedule. Unless something (or someone) intervenes, Mordecai may well be dead by the time of the banquet, and thus "ineligible" for the reprieve. Esther cannot possibly intervene for him *before* the banquet because she knows nothing of Haman's plans. (They were hatched, remember, in the privacy of his home and due to be enacted first thing in the morning.) If ever there was a moment for *deus ex machina*, this is it.

Enter the coincidences. Granted, they are not in the same league as the burning bush or the parting of the Red Sea. What they lack in dramatic flair, however, they more than make up for in effectiveness. And they are entirely consistent with God's "behind the scenes" role in this story (see Introduction, pp. 13–14).

Just as the king begins to ponder his obvious oversight with regard to Mordecai's reward, something catches his eye out in the court (v. 4). What a coincidence! It is Haman, who seems to be having a sleepless night himself. Psalm 36:1–4 could well have been written about him:

> Transgression speaks to the wicked deep in their hearts;
>   there is no fear of God before their eyes.
> For they flatter themselves in their own eyes
>   that their iniquity cannot be found out and hated.
> The words of their mouths are mischief and deceit;
>   they have ceased to act wisely and do good.
> They plot mischief while on their beds;
>   they are set on a way that is not good;
>   they do not reject evil.

There is wonderful irony in the fact that, if Haman had not been so anxious to get the king's permission to impale Mordecai, he would never have been on hand for his own humiliation. Yet there he is, ready to risk perhaps as much as Esther did in coming to the king uninvited, and about to receive the biggest surprise of his life. Fortunately—or unfortunately—for him, Ahasuerus calls him in.

Esther 6:6–9
Delusions of Grandeur

The king is so preoccupied that he does not stop to ask Haman the obvious question, namely, "What do you want?" Instead, he blurts out the question that eclipses all else: "What shall be done for the man whom the king wishes to honor?" (v. 6a).

Anyone with a modicum of modesty (or sense) would have stopped to wonder about that question. But Haman apparently has neither, and immediately assumes that *he* is the one the king wishes to honor. This self-aggrandizing assumption sets up the comedy of errors that follows. "Whom would the king wish to honor more than me?" he asks, with the flawless logic of a megalomaniac.

Just as the king is preoccupied with how to honor Mordecai, so Haman is now preoccupied with how to honor himself. Their mutual preoccupation makes for hilarious misunderstanding. The humor hinges on the fact that the readers know more than either of the characters do. It is a comic device that has served authors well for centuries and never fails to delight (though usually at the characters' expense). Like Beatrice and Benedick in *Much Ado About Nothing*, or Abbott and Costello in *Who's On First?*, Haman and Ahasuerus are having a conversation that only their audience really understands.

The alacrity with which Haman comes up with the ideas in verses 7 through 9 suggests that he has entertained this fantasy before. "Let royal robes be brought," he suggests helpfully, "which the king has worn, and a horse that the king has ridden, with a royal crown on its head" (v. 8). The first thing to strike a modern reader is the absurdity of a horse wearing a crown, and we are likely to assume that Haman is really going "over the top" here. There are some difficulties with the Hebrew syntax, however, that leave open the possibility that it is the honoree who is supposed to wear the crown and not the horse. (The LXX leaves the phrase out altogether.) Yet, even if it is the horse that is wearing the crown, we ought not to assume that this is as ridiculous as it seems. Such could have been a part of the royal steed's accoutrements (Moore, *Esther*, 65, but see also Beal, 83; cf. v. 11). Either way, the important thing to note is the height of Haman's ambitions. To wear the king's own clothing and to ride the king's horse was to have the power of the king himself (see 1 Kgs. 1:33 where David has Solomon ride the former's own mule to the latter's coronation). Haman already has Ahasuerus's signet ring (3:10); these additional items would represent a virtual clean sweep. The only "thing" Haman would lack would be the queen (see 7:8).

The fantasy gets better and better. In verse 9 Haman urges Ahasuerus to appoint "one of the king's most noble officials" to act as valet, escort, and herald, robing the honoree and leading him on horseback through the most public parts of the city proclaiming that this is how the king treats those he wishes to honor. Haman is clearly on a roll. "This," we can imagine him musing as he pauses for breath, "is going to be great."

Esther 6:10–14

Haman's Waking Nightmare

Whether Haman has finished with his fantasy or not, dream soon turns to waking nightmare as Ahasuerus interrupts with the words

Haman never expected to hear. "Quickly," the king orders, "take the robes and the horse, as you have said, and do so to the Jew Mordecai who sits at the king's gate. Leave out nothing that you have mentioned" (v. 10). To say that Haman probably regrets having been quite so free with his suggestions would be an obvious understatement. Yet the reality check could not be more abrupt. A second ago he was imagining himself as the most powerful person in the Persian Empire. Now, he is taking orders like any other lackey in the realm . . . and odious orders at that.

Ahasuerus must think it handy that just such a high-ranking official is present to serve as Mordecai's escort. After all, Mordecai's reward has waited long enough (2:3). Yet it is interesting that Ahasuerus does not seem to notice the incongruity (!) of honoring a condemned man. This raises a couple of questions about the extent of the king's knowledge (and perhaps his intelligence). Is he too dense to realize the irony, or is he simply unaware that Mordecai is one of the people condemned by Haman's edict? A close comparison of Ahasuerus's words here and Haman's words in chapter 3 suggests the latter.

According to 6:10, the king is aware that Mordecai is a Jew, and that he is a frequent figure at the gate of the palace. In Haman's original argument before Ahasuerus in 3:8, however, Haman never specifies that this "certain people" who so offend him are the Jews. While the written edict states this quite specifically, the oral argument never does. It would seem, therefore, that Ahasuerus has never heard nor seen an actual copy of the edict that he gave Haman permission to write. He does not know, therefore, that it is the Jews who are implicated in the edict, and thus that Mordecai is under a death sentence. So, although Ahasuerus may be a relatively "dim bulb," the problem here has more to do with limited knowledge rather than limited intelligence. These limits underscore two things we have noted before: first, the power of the written text, and second, the isolation of the palace.

Haman does his duty and carries out every jot and tittle of the king's command (v. 11). We can well imagine how hateful this is for him, and indeed, the narrative tells us that after it was over "Haman hurried to his house, mourning and with his head covered" (v. 12). The narrative tells us nothing, however, about how Mordecai felt about the experience. Surely, the irony was not lost on him! We are told only that he "returned to the king's gate." Perhaps this was the only avenue that seemed possible to him under the circumstances. A party, after all, would hardly have been appropriate. However sweet the taste of his temporary exaltation over his archenemy Haman, it must have been bittersweet in light of the edict.

Haman's fan club is less than comforting when Haman tells them "everything that had happened to him" (v.13). In fact, they seem to waste no time in distancing themselves from him. Note, for instance, their use of the second-person singular in their gloomy analysis of the day's events: "If Mordecai, before whom *your* downfall has begun, is of the Jewish people, *you* will not prevail against him, but will surely fall before him" (italics mine). So much for "We're all in this together."

The words of Haman's wife and advisors also comprise an awkward confession of faith. The motif of the "foreigner's confession" is not that uncommon in the Bible. Several stories come to mind as examples: Balaam's ass in Numbers 22; the terrified sailors in Jonah 1:14; the unclean spirit in Mark 1:23–24; or the centurion at the crucifixion in Matthew 27:54; Mark 15:39; and Luke 23:47. Although Haman's supporters never actually confess their faith in the God of the Jews, they seem to have a kind of superstitious sense of the Jews' superiority (cf. the views of the servants in 3:3). They had, of course, neglected to mention any of their reservations earlier. When Haman made his initial complaint to them about "the Jew Mordecai," they were only too happy to urge Haman on. The tide, however, has turned against Haman, and they seem only too anxious to abandon ship.

Given the pace of the narrative at this point, they had better hurry. Even as they speak, the ubiquitous eunuchs arrive to hurry Haman off to the banquet (v. 14; see also 1:10–12, where the eunuchs come to fetch Vashti). This makes the third overt reference to speedy action in recent verses (see also vv. 10 and 12). Circumstances seem to have conspired against Haman, and for once, we get the impression he is completely unprepared. Esther, however, is not. The chapter closes with a reference to the banquet that she has prepared. We can be sure that her preparations involve far more than food.

PART SEVEN

ESTHER 7

Esther 7:1–6
Esther Argues Her Case

Chapter 6 practically treads on the heels of chapter 7 as the plot hurtles forward right along with Haman. Things are very much out of control now from his perspective. While there is no clue as to what he is thinking as the eunuchs bear him off to the banquet (6:14), readers may recall the last time the eunuchs were sent to summon someone to a banquet. Things did not turn out well for Vashti (1:10–11). Together with the pace of the narrative and the grim predictions of Haman's wife and friends (6:13), this parallel adds to our sense of the inexorability of Haman's defeat.

He is not dead yet, however. As the king and Haman arrive at the feast (7:1), all eyes are trained on Esther as we wait for her to state her case. Two questions crowd to the foreground. First, will she do it? She has, after all, backed down or thought better of it twice before (5:4 and 5:8). Second, if she does at last seize the moment, how will she craft her argument?

Before we consider her case, however, we need to take stock of her timing. If we thought that Esther missed the perfect moment when she passed up her chance to reveal her request at the first banquet (5:6–7), providence has accommodated her here with an even more advantageous one. Once again the wine is flowing, suggesting the king's receptivity. Indeed, there is slightly more emphasis on alcohol in this chapter, with the usual word for "banquet" being replaced in verse 1 with a word that is usually associated with drinking (the NRSV translates it "feast"). Remember, too, all that has transpired in the interim. Ahasuerus has Mordecai's loyalty fresh in his mind. Haman has erected a six-story stake on which to impale Mordecai. (This circumstantial evidence will not go over well in a moment.) And finally, Haman is almost certainly rattled. His experience of having to honor his worst enemy publicly has to have affected his emotional equilibrium. From Esther's perspective, then, it is prime time.

Right on cue, Ahasuerus repeats his question: "What is your petition . . . And what is your request?" Esther is ready. This time, her introduction is leaner and slightly more familiar. "If I have won your favor, O king," she begins, "and if it pleases the king . . ." Then she cuts straight to the chase:

> let my life be given me—that is my petition—
> and the lives of my people—that is my request.

Further arguments follow, but this opening statement is worthy of immediate comment. Esther takes advantage of Ahasuerus's two-part question (almost poetic in its parallelism) to line out the parallels between herself and her people. This connection is critical and must be made with the utmost clarity. Ahasuerus needs to understand that he can no longer view the queen as an individual or a personal possession, but as part of a larger entity.

Notice, too, that Esther resists the temptation to "bury the lead" (to borrow a phrase from journalism). A less carefully crafted statement might have begun with the story of how Haman had taken offense at Mordecai and sought the destruction of the Jews as an outgrowth of his personal vendetta, and so forth. While such an approach would have made sense in terms of sequence, it would not have been nearly as effective. By leading with these lines, Esther makes sure the king understands that her life has been threatened. Her words both shock and inform. One suspects they may have sobered the king up a bit in the bargain.

Esther moves quickly to her explanation. "For we have been sold," she says, "I and my people, to be destroyed, to be killed, and to be annihilated. If we had been sold merely as slaves, men and women, I would have held my peace; but no enemy can compensate for this damage to the king" (v. 4).

Esther's references to being sold into slavery seem like a non sequitur unless one understands the play on words discussed in chapter 3. While it is possible to understand her reference to being "sold" as a kind of figurative flourish (perhaps along the lines of being "sold out" as in Deut. 32:30 or Judg. 4:9), or as an allusion to the money Haman offers the king for their destruction in 3:9, there is another explanation that makes rather more sense and has the added advantage of recognizing Esther's rhetorical skill. Let us briefly review the issues introduced in chapter 3 (pp. 42–43).

In Haman's original proposal to Ahasuerus, remember, he asked that an edict be issued for a certain people's "destruction" (3:9). This seems utterly straightforward, until one realizes that the word for "destruction" (from the root *ʾābad*) sounds almost exactly like the word for "enslavement" (from the root *ʿābad*). Sandra Beth Berg raises the possibility that while the text says "destruction," Ahasuerus may have heard "enslavement," since the words are virtual homophones (101–3; compare especially *lĕ ʾabdām* in 3:9 with *la ʿăbādîm* in 7:4). Haman's offer to pay such a significant sum of money could well have encouraged the king toward such a conclusion.

All ambiguity is eliminated in the written text of the edict, however, which specifies not only that the Jews be destroyed, but that they be killed and annihilated as well (3:13). Thus, what may have been uncertain at the oral level is made painfully plain in writing.

When we bear this discussion in mind, Esther's argument in chapter 7 makes much more sense. She begins by saying, "For we have been sold . . ." (v. 4). In doing so she starts where Ahasuerus is. If he is under the impression that he has "merely" sold a group of his subjects into slavery, for example, this way of beginning may help him make the connection between that decision and her situation. Yet, by qualifying this with the next phrase, "to be destroyed, to be killed, and to be annihilated," she diplomatically points out that he has been duped. (Note how this phrase is an exact quote of the written edict.)

Her next statement almost apologizes for having brought this to Ahasuerus's attention. "If we had been sold merely as slaves, men and women," she says, "I would have held my peace; but no enemy can compensate for this damage to the king." Note the way in which her reference to this yet unnamed "enemy" turns the attention off the delicate topic of the king's misapprehension toward the one who tricked him. It also anticipates any objection the king might raise about the potential loss of revenue by implying that no amount of money would make such a loss worthwhile. Finally, Esther's words characterize the plot as an affront to the king, and not as "just" a threat to herself or her people. Given Ahasuerus's vanity, this could well be her most important point.

Before we move on to consider Ahasuerus's reaction, we ought to pause for a moment to consider again, "What does the queen know, and when does she know it?" The shape of Esther's argument here suggests two things. First, it argues strongly for the "homophone" confusion in chapter 3. She capitalizes on the king's confusion and crafts her argument in light of it. Yet it also suggests that she has done her homework. Sometime between Haman's initial conversation with the king in chapter 3, and her present conversation with Ahasuerus in this chapter, she has figured out how the king has been tricked. We know that she has seen the written text of the edict because the narrator tells us so in 4:8 and because she quotes it in this passage ("to be destroyed, to be killed, and to be annihilated"). Yet her words here also seem to reflect the ambiguities of the oral argument. Thus, we can be fairly sure of "what" the queen knows. "When" she discovered it is less certain, in that we can only deduce that it was sometime between the original conversation and the present one. Completely uncertain, however, is "how" she came by her information. She, like Mordecai, seems to have her sources. (The ubiquitous eunuchs come to mind.) Yet, "how" is not as important as "that." The important thing is that she has done her research and that she has used it to craft a brilliant case. The only question remaining is: Will it work?

It can work only if Ahasuerus "gets it." In verse 5, it is not clear that he does. His words indicate that he is beginning to catch on to the fact that he's been duped, but that he still has not made the connection to Haman. Picking up on Esther's reference to an "enemy," he blusters, "Who is he, and where is he, who has presumed to do this?" To help him make this last crucial connection, Esther spells it out for him in verse 6 by declaring, "A foe and enemy, this wicked Haman!" Her words recognize that Haman is their common enemy (as compared to 3:10 where he was identified only as the enemy of the Jews). Sensing this new and formidable alliance, Haman is understandably "terrified before the king and the queen" (6b).

Esther 7:7–10
Crime and Punishment

Ahasuerus chooses this pivotal moment to storm out into the palace garden. (Perhaps he is trying to control his characteristic rage, or perhaps he simply needs a moment to rearrange his perception of reality.) Haman, however, is absolutely clear about the implications of this new reality and acts decisively. Seeing "that the king had determined to destroy him," he stays to "beg his life from Queen Esther" (v. 7). There is both symmetry and irony in the fact that the word translated as "beg" is the same one that is behind the noun "request," which we have seen in the king's repeated question to Esther (5:3, 6; 7:2). Now it is Haman's turn to plead for his life. It is interesting that he assumes Esther has the power to grant it to him. And it is astonishing that he hopes she has the inclination!

Unfortunately for Haman, Ahasuerus returns to the room just in time to see Haman throwing himself on the couch where Queen Esther is reclining (v. 8). (Could this be another stroke of providence?) *We* know that Haman is throwing himself upon her mercy as much as her couch. Ahasuerus jumps to other conclusions, however, and asks incredulously, "Will he even assault the queen in my presence, in my own house?" Even as the king misunderstands, Haman again understands. In a wonderfully vivid metaphor, the narrator tells us that "as the words left the mouth of the king, they covered Haman's face."

A decision is obviously in order. Yet, as we have seen previously (1:2; 2:4), Ahasuerus is ever open to suggestion at such moments. This time it is Harbona the eunuch who gets to advise the king and pronounce Haman's highly appropriate sentence. "Look," Harbona points out helpfully, "the very gallows that Haman has prepared for Mordecai, whose word saved the king, stands at Haman's house, fifty cubits high" (v. 9).

There is a sense in which Haman is condemned here by the excesses of his own ego. The extravagant height of the stake in Haman's back yard (see the discussion on p. 55 as to whether the instrument of execution is a gallows or a stake) is visible even from the palace. Freshly inspired by the sight, Ahasuerus issues his first direct order in the entire book. "Hang him on that," he says, and the servants are quick to comply.

The irony here, of course, is that Haman is ultimately punished for a crime he did not commit. He was not, after all, assaulting the queen. Yet perhaps Ahasuerus's conclusions were not as false as they first appeared, nor he as dense. Remember, after all, Haman's fantasy in chapter 6 about wearing the king's clothes and riding the king's horse. And he already had the king's signet ring, after all (3:10). Perhaps Ahasuerus remembered these things during his "time-out" in the garden. In light of them, Haman's apparent assault on the queen may have looked like the next logical step in a well-planned coup (cf. Absalom's "appropriation" of David's concubines in 2 Sam. 16:20–22). In any case, Ahasuerus finally makes a decision, and Haman is summarily dispatched to his doom (v. 10). Only this is enough to quiet the anger of the king.

Verse 10 makes a point of the fact that Haman is finally impaled on the stake "that he had prepared for Mordecai." Thus, he is "hoist with his own petard" and we share Hamlet's satisfaction in the symmetry (Shakespeare's *Hamlet*, III, IV, 214). Yet this chapter contains an even more important element of symmetry that we should not miss.

Back in chapter 3 when Haman first made his immodest proposal to the king, we commented on his having reached the level of "evil genius." He is not simply wicked, but brilliant, deceitful, and highly efficient as well. Thus, we wondered whether he would ever meet his match. Could anyone possibly arise who could outwit him, matching every ounce of his evil with good?

In chapters 5 and 7, Esther's character rises to that occasion. She is patient in implementing her plan of attack. She is brilliant in her analysis of her enemy's methods. And finally, she is every bit his equal in her power to persuade. Esther's character is so strong by the end of this chapter that we almost begin to feel sorry for Haman. But not quite. In the words of Jane Austen—another author famous for her strong female characters—Haman has "delighted us long enough" (*Pride and Prejudice*, chap. 18). We are glad to see him go.

PART EIGHT

ESTHER 8

Esther 8:1–8

Just Deserts

Ahasuerus has had a full day. It began with a bout of insomnia (6:1). Then came the discovery of Mordecai's unrewarded loyalty, followed by the misconstrued consultation with Haman (6:2–9). Perhaps he caught a nap during the parade (6:10–11), but he is back at the banquet by the beginning of chapter 7. The banquet was pleasant enough, but then there was that exhausting scene with Haman, culminating, of course, with the "attack" on the queen and the necessity of having Haman executed.

Yet Ahasuerus's day is not over. There is still much to be done. In fact, if one were to designate a theme for this day it might be "just deserts." Mordecai, after all, had finally gotten what he deserved for saving the king's life. Haman definitely got what was coming to him when he was stripped of both his life and his honor. Now on a decision-making roll, Ahasuerus continues to try to redress past injustices.

He begins by giving Haman's house to Queen Esther (8:1). What could be more fitting from the king's perspective? Haman had wronged the queen in two ways, both by plotting her death and assaulting her person. And while Haman had tried to trick Ahasuerus, Esther had unveiled his perfidy. She clearly deserves some compensation for her pains.

Mordecai, too, has earned some additional reward. The parade was fine for recognizing his role in scuttling the assassination attempt, but now Esther has acknowledged him as her uncle. This means that he, too, was the target of Haman's treachery. If Esther's explanation went beyond the mere basics of their relationship, then Ahasuerus must also know that Mordecai was Haman's particular target. What better reward for him than the king's own signet ring, recently retrieved from the unfortunate Haman's finger (v. 2)?

One would think that recent experience might give the king pause before handing over his signet ring again. Yet he seems almost anxious to get rid of it. Perhaps it is connected to his tendency to let others influence—or even make—his decisions (1:13–22; 2:1–4; 3:7–11). In any case,

it is hardly on his hand again before he removes it and gives it to Mordecai. At least Mordecai is a better choice. He has proven to be a trustwor-
thy servant with the king's best interests at heart. Maybe the king's
judgment is improving. In any case, Mordecai's possession of the signet
ring is a fact that will figure heavily in the resolution of the story's conflict.

The focus shifts to Esther at the end of verse 2. It is her turn to
make some decisions now. The first is to appoint Mordecai to run her
newly acquired house. There is a sweet symmetry in this detail given
the bitter animosity that has characterized the relationship between
those two men throughout the story. In a sense, it is the last imbalance
to be rectified at the level of the individual characters.

Yet this is not just a story about individuals; the fate of a whole people hangs in the balance. Esther's next act recognizes this. Verse 3
reflects her decision to speak to the king again, this time falling at his
feet, "weeping and pleading with him to avert the evil design of Haman
the Agagite and the plot that he had devised against the Jews."

The first thing to note about this is her manner. Never before has
Esther stated her case in such a dramatic—even melodramatic—fashion. As we shall see subsequently, she is still capable of a tightly controlled argument. Yet her opening statement is in stark contrast to the
stately introduction to her last speech (7:3). What is behind this sudden
and passionate outburst?

There is no indication of how much time passes between the end
of verse 2 and the beginning of verse 3. The text does say that "Esther
spoke *again* to the king," however, which would seem to indicate that
what follows is a separate conversation from what has gone before (v. 3;
italics mine). This impression is reinforced by the fact that the king
holds out the golden scepter to her again (v. 4). Although the narrative
does not dwell on this detail as it has before (4:11; 5:2), the reader is by
this time well aware of the risk that Esther runs in initiating another
interview. In any case, there seems to be some sort of intermission—
though possibly brief—between these two verses.

This is significant only because it may offer an explanation for
Esther's change in tone. There is a kind of "all's well that ends well" feel-
ing at the end of verse 2. Perhaps Ahasuerus thinks he has done enough
for one day, or indeed, has done all that needs to be done. Esther has
Haman's house, after all, and Mordecai has the king's own signet ring.
What more could they want?

The flaw in this logic would be appallingly obvious to Esther. First
of all, Haman's house is not going to be much good to her after the thirteenth of Adar (the date the edict is due to go into effect). Similarly, the
signet ring will not mean much to Mordecai if he is dead. Both of these

69

observations simply call attention to the fact that the real crisis here is not individual, but corporate. Haman may be dead, but his edict lives on. In less than nine months' time, the Jews are due to die. This real and present danger more than accounts for the queen's rising level of desperation. By expressly referring to "Haman the Agagite and the plot that he had devised against the Jews," she calls Ahasuerus's attention to the corporate nature of the crisis.

Having thus reminded him of the necessity to do more, she then proceeds to make some diplomatic suggestions (v. 5). Abandoning her suppliant position, she rises and stands before Ahasuerus. This time four qualifying phrases preface her request, all designed to reinforce the king's sense that he is ultimately in charge. If Esther resents that fact, she at least does a better job of hiding it than Haman did. Contrast, for instance, her contingent "if the thing seems right before the king" with Haman's presumptuous "it is not appropriate for the king to tolerate them" (3:8). Esther uses every word, even in polite formalities, to advance her cause. Once these preliminary phrases are milked for their full effect, Esther makes her proposal:

> Let an order be written to revoke the letters devised by Haman son of Hammedatha the Agagite, which he wrote giving orders to destroy the Jews who are in all the provinces of the king.

This request reflects at least as much rhetorical skill as her first one (7:3–4). Notice, for instance, that she assigns blame solely to Haman. While one could easily make a case for the king's passive culpability, it would hardly be wise to hint at that now. Second, she reminds Ahasuerus that there is a property issue at stake. Although this may sound crass, she can hardly count on his humanitarian instincts. The threatened Jews are "in all the provinces of the king," and thus their destruction could be construed as a valuable loss of property. Finally, in describing the letters as "devised" by Haman, she may be referring to the deceitful tactics that Haman employed to get the edict passed in the first place (cf. 9:24 and 25). What better grounds could there be for revoking Haman's edict than that it was passed under false pretenses?

Verse 6 continues her argument, but in a more personal and emotional vein. "How can I bear to see the calamity that is coming on my people?" she asks. "Or how can I bear to see the destruction of my kindred?" (cf. Heb. 1:13).

At no point in the book is Esther's complete identification with her people more strongly stated. This outburst puts to rest any lingering doubts that may have been planted by Mordecai's remark in chapter 4: "Do not think that in the king's palace you will escape any more than all

70

the other Jews" (4:13). Here, Esther's focus is entirely on the fate of her people; she does not even bother to argue for herself. Her words may even be intended to short-circuit any attempt on the king's part to spare her and let the people die. In any case, these rhetorical questions are her last, best attempt to make Ahasuerus understand that she and her people are one. If he cares about her—and this verse suggests her sense that he does—then he must do something about Haman's edict.

Ahasuerus's reply, issued jointly "to Queen Esther and to the Jew Mordecai," is disappointing in the extreme (vv. 7–8). It is as if he has not even heard Esther's arguments. "I have given Esther the house of Haman," he reiterates, and Haman himself has been executed "because he plotted to lay hands on the Jews." Continuing to retrace his steps (see v. 2), he then refers to the signet ring, suggesting to Esther and Mordecai, "You (plural) may write as you please with regard to the Jews, in the name of the king, and seal it with the king's ring." But why should they have to write anything new, we wonder? Esther did not ask for a new edict, after all, but for a revocation of the old one. Then the king drops a bombshell: "For an edict written in the name of the king and sealed with the king's ring cannot be revoked."

Now we are truly incredulous about how free Ahasuerus has been with his signet ring. What is this all about?

Alert readers may remember one other passing reference to the apparent inflexibility of "the laws of the Persians and the Medes." With regard to the law about Vashti's banishment, Memucan says, "If it pleases the king, let a royal order go out from him, and let it be written among the laws of the Persians and the Medes *so that it may not be altered*" (1:19; italics mine). On closer examination, however, this verse may not bear so strongly on the present passage as it seems. The word translated as "altered" is from the root *ʿābar*, which might better be translated as "pass away" or even "be passed over." This is the sense in which it is used later in the book (9:27 and 28) in the context of observing the two days of Purim. The idea in 1:19 is that the law should be written down so that it will not fall into disuse (see esp. 9:28). One suspects that the NRSV's translation in 1:19 may be a bit too much "under the influence" of 8:8 at this point.

The issue in 8:5 and 8 is whether or not an edict written in the name of the king and sealed with his ring may be *revoked* (*šūb*). To be fair to Ahasuerus, we have to assume that there was such a rule (though it is tempting to think he may have just misunderstood Memucan's words in 1:19; it would not be the first time he got confused over something someone has said, after all). The existence of such a law does put his previous reticence in a new and slightly more flattering light. Perhaps

71

it was not because he *would* not do more for the Jews, but because he felt he *could* not do more for them.

It should be pointed out that Daniel 6:9 and 13 do reflect this irrevocability rule. Levenson points out, however, that there is no extrabiblical evidence for the policy, and further approves Fox's assessment that it seems "an impossible way to run an empire" (Levenson, 52; Fox, 22). My own view is that in both Daniel and Esther the rule is more of a plot device than a reflection of historical reality. In any case, it is a real and present danger for the purposes of this narrative, and must be taken at face value.

Esther, evidently, did not know about this rule when she asked in verse 5 that "an order be written to revoke (*šūb*) the letters devised by Haman." Or she may simply have thought the rule was inapplicable since, as we suggested earlier, Haman's edict was passed under false pretenses. Whether she knew or not, the notion that Haman's edict might be invalid presents the perfect logical loophole for the "irrevocability clause." If she makes this hint, however, Ahasuerus is either too rigid or too unimaginative to get it. The only solution he can see is a counteredict. He is certainly unimaginative about that, leaving it to Esther and Mordecai to write their way out of the bind into which he has helped place them.

More striking even than Ahasuerus's lack of imagination is his lack of power. One cannot help but compare the "Mighty Man" of the book's introduction with the weak and ineffectual monarch pictured here. Remember, though, that the signs of his weakness were showing early on. In chapter 1, after all, he could not call his wife; in chapter 8 he cannot save her. Indeed, one wonders whether he has even grasped the necessity of saving her. His words, "You may write as you please with regard to the Jews," sound almost offhand, as if he still does not quite understand that his wife is Jewish.

One thing, at least, is clear. Esther and Mordecai cannot rely on Ahasuerus for much help. The words of a dead traitor have proven more powerful than the commands of a living king. Their only option seems to be to fight fire with fire—edict with edict.

Esther 8:9–16

Mordecai's Balancing Act

Esther evidently gives Mordecai sole responsibility for dictating the counteredict. Although the king had used the second-person plural

in saying "You may write as you please with regard to the Jews" (v. 8), the edict described in verse 9 is written "according to all that Mordecai commanded." While no motive is given for this delegation of responsibility, it does have the effect of making comparisons cleaner. This is good, because the passage describing the second edict invites several salient comparisons.

Everything about the language of verses 9 through 14 echoes earlier descriptions of "mass mailings." Compare, for instance, this phrase

1:22	*8:9*
. . . he sent letters to all the royal provinces, to every province in its own script and to every people in its own language . . .	. . . one hundred twenty-seven provinces, to every province in its own script and to every people in its own language

from 8:9 with the description of the mailing in chapter 1 ordering that "every man should be master in his own house":

The most marked similarities and differences, however, are with the description of Haman's edict in chapter 3. Although the parallels are even more striking in Hebrew, the NRSV's English translation is close enough to preserve the echoes in the original.

3:12–15a	*8:9–14*
Then the king's secretaries were summoned	The king's secretaries were summoned at that time,
on the thirteenth day of the first month	in the third month, which is the month of Sivan, on the twenty-third day;
and an edict,	and an edict was written,
according to all that Haman commanded,	according to all that Mordecai commanded,
was written to the king's satraps	to the Jews and to the satraps
and to the governors over all the provinces	and the governors
and to the officials of all the peoples,	and the officials of the provinces
	from India to Ethiopia,
	one hundred twenty-seven provinces
to every province in its own script	to every province in its own script
and every people in its own language;	and to every people in its own language,
	and also to the Jews in their script
	and their language.
it was written in the name of King Ahasuerus	He wrote letters in the name of King Ahasuerus,
and sealed with the king's ring.	sealed them with the king's ring,
Letters were sent by couriers	and sent them by mounted couriers riding on fast steeds bred from the royal herd.
to all the king's provinces,	By these letters the king allowed the Jews who were in every city to assemble and defend their lives,
giving orders to destroy, to kill, and to annihilate	to destroy, to kill, and to annihilate
all Jews, young and old,	any armed force of any people or province that might attack them,

73

women and children, in one day,	with their children and women, and to plunder their goods on a single day throughout all the provinces of King Ahasuerus,
the thirteenth day of the twelfth month, which is the month of Adar, and to plunder their goods.	on the thirteenth day of the twelfth month which is the month of Adar.
A copy of the document was to be issued as a decree in every province by proclamation, calling on all the peoples to be ready for that day.	A copy of the writ was to be issued as a decree in every province and published to all peoples, and the Jews were to be ready on that day to take revenge on their enemies.
The couriers went quickly	So the couriers, mounted on their swift royal steeds, hurried out,
by order of the king, and the decree was issued in the citadel of Susa.	urged by the king's command. The decree was issued in the citadel of Susa.

The first thing that is obvious from this comparison is that Mordecai does not view the authorship of the counteredict as an exercise in creative writing. The narrative description of the composition, content, and publication of this second edict underscores that it is very much modeled on the first one. Every element of the first edict finds its counterpart in the second. This is extraordinarily important for understanding this passage. It is not so much that Mordecai is anxious "to destroy, to kill, and to annihilate," but rather, that the second edict must counteract the first. Every detail is designed with a restoration of balance in mind. Remember, as well, that Esther and Mordecai's first choice would have been to revoke Haman's edict entirely, thus obviating any need for violence. Failing that, the counteredict at least tries to ensure that it is a fair fight.

The differences between the two edicts are every bit as revealing as the similarities. Several of these differences may be seen by carefully contrasting 8:11 with 3:13. Mordecai's edict, for instance, gives *permission* to destroy, kill, annihilate, and plunder, while Haman's edict gives *orders* for the same. Mordecai's edict is framed in terms of self-defense, while Haman's is undisguised aggression. Note as well that Mordecai's edict specifies that violence be used in response to "any armed force of any people or province that might attack them," while Haman's edict directs the violence against the general Jewish population, including women and children.

The issue of whether the Jews are also given permission to kill their enemies' women and children should perhaps receive special comment. There is certainly one way of reading 8:11 which assumes that permission is being given *both* to kill "their children and women and to

74

plunder their goods." This reading has symmetry on its side, since as we have pointed out, each element of the first edict is matched by a counterpart in the second. Another consideration that may support this is the idea of the ritual ban (*ḥērem*), a practice by which both the lives and the property of an enemy are "dedicated to God." Failure to comply with this practice was, after all, the very thing that got Saul into trouble with Haman's ancestor Agag in 1 Samuel 15. (For a summary of that story's relevance to this one, see p. 36; cf. Levenson, 110–11.) Although one hates to argue in favor of this reading for obvious reasons, one can make a case for it.

There is, however, another way of reading verse 11 that has at least as many facts in its favor. The first is this verse's own focus on "any armed force," which as we argued earlier, is in contrast to the general scope of the first edict. Equally persuasive, however, is the placement of the verse divider in the Hebrew text, which allows one to read the verse this way: "to destroy, to kill, and to annihilate any armed force of any people or province that might attack them with their children and women—and to plunder their goods." The assumption here, then, is that it is the *Jewish* women and children that are being attacked and not the Persian ones. If this is the case, then the mention of the children and women in this verse would be *in contrast* with its use in the first edict, perhaps heightening the sense that the Jews are to act in self-defense. Note, also, that while they are given express permission to plunder their enemies' goods, they do not in fact do so (9:10, 15, and 16).

Two more contrasts between the two edicts are worth mentioning. The first has to do with the second edict's being sent expressly "to the Jews" as well as "the satraps and the governors and the officials" (v. 9). Later in the same verse, notice the addition of the words "and also to the Jews in their script and their language," after the usual list of recipients. It seems incredible that the very people being condemned by the first edict should be left off the otherwise exhaustive list, but perhaps that is what is implied here. In any case, Mordecai is not taking any chances that they will not receive the news of the second one!

Finally, the modus operandi is significantly more efficient in the delivery of the second edict. While Haman's edict was sent out by mere "couriers" (3:13), Mordecai's edict goes out on "mounted couriers riding on fast steeds bred from the royal herd" (8:10). A second reference to this Persian pony express comes in verse 14, which reads, "So the couriers, mounted on their swift royal steeds, hurried out, urged by the king's command." (Note that at last Ahasuerus is of some help!) It is interesting that while Mordecai may not have felt free to be very cre-

75

ative in the composition of the edict, he does not feel so constrained with regard to its delivery.

Having compared and contrasted the two edicts, we ought also to compare and contrast the responses to them. While the language does not line up as exactly as in the previous passages, the similarities and differences are still striking. After the first edict, the king and Haman sit down to drink (3:15). After the second, Haman is noticeably absent, and it is the Jews who are having a celebratory drink (the word translated as "festival" in 8:17 implies that there was drinking). Pandemonium breaks out in the city of Susa in response to both edicts, but the confusion is characterized by shouts of joy in the latter instance. Mordecai dons sackcloth and ashes after the first, but is royally arrayed after the second. Finally, the Jews become increasingly isolated in the aftermath of the first edict. After the second, however, they can hardly count the converts—sincere or otherwise (8:17).

There is still an element of fear at the end of this chapter. The thirteenth of Adar, after all, still looms large. The difference is that it now looms large for the Persians, too.

Modern Christians may read this "good news" with mixed emotions. We neither can nor should forget Jesus' words about turning the other cheek and loving our enemies. Yet we must also try to read this story on its own terms even as we also read it within its broader canonical context. Crucial to the latter is the recognition that violence was not Esther and Mordecai's first choice. The second edict is a second choice, and a very limited one at that. Life will certainly be lost—on both sides. But with the publication of the second edict, Mordecai has at least restored a balance to the situation. Given their previous vulnerability in the midst of a hostile and unjust environment, that is no small feat.

Believers in every age must make such choices. In a post-Holocaust world, we can no longer pretend that they will be easy. Even Dietrich Bonhoeffer decided to fight back, after all, when faced with the horrors perpetrated by the Nazis. The words to the hymn text he wrote a year before he was hanged by his enemies testify to the excruciating nature of the choice:

> Yet is this heart by its old foe tormented,
> Still evil days bring burdens hard to bear
> O give our frightened souls the sure salvation
> For which, O Lord, You taught us to prepare.
> (from "By Gracious Powers," stanza 2)

It is surely significant that his words are framed as a prayer.

ESTHER 9 AND 10

Esther 9:1–19
A War of Words

Back in chapter 3, Mordecai's fellow servants wondered whether his words would avail against Haman (3:4). That, as it turns out, is the central question of the book. Edict is now pitted against edict. All that remains is to see whose words will prove to be more powerful.

The only hint we have had in the nine-month hiatus between the end of the last chapter and the beginning of this one are the words "because the fear of the Jews had fallen upon them" (8:17). This nameless dread has peeked around the edges of Persian comments before. It is evident—at least in the guise of nervous curiosity— in the passage from 3:4 quoted above. Yet it is most obvious in the words of Haman's wife and friends who predicted that "If Mordecai, before whom your downfall has begun, is of the Jewish people, you will not prevail against him, but will surely fall before him" (6:13).

As the battle finally begins, however, this fear surges to the surface and becomes a veritable epidemic of dread. Indeed, it is credited with the victory. When the Jews gather throughout the land to defend themselves against their attackers, "no one could withstand them" says verse 2, "because the fear of them had fallen upon all peoples." The epidemic is no respecter of rank, either. Verse 3 describes its effect on the various government officials, who suddenly swing their support to the Jews because "the fear of Mordecai had fallen upon them." (So much for party loyalty.)

The fact that it is this fear that tips the balance and allows the great reversal described in verse 1 may be one more instance of God's low-profile role in this book. While it is true that God's name is not actually mentioned here or elsewhere, there are moments when the outcome is heavily dependent on something beyond the control of the characters (see the discussion on pp. 13–14 re other instances of "divine coincidence"). There is a sense in which "relief and deliverance" has arisen here for the Jews "from another quarter" (4:14). One can easily imagine Psalm 124 on their lips at the end of the day:

> If it had not been the LORD who was on our side . . .
> . . . when our enemies attacked us
> then they would have swallowed us up alive . . .
> Blessed be the LORD
> who has not given us as prey to their teeth.
> We have escaped like a bird from the snare of the fowlers;
> the snare is broken, and we have escaped.
> Our help is in the name of the LORD,
> who made heaven and earth.
>
> (Psalm 124:1–2, 6–8)

That there is a dramatic reversal described here cannot be disputed. The tension in verse 1 is heart stopping. On the dreaded day "when the king's command and edict were about to be executed," it says, giving one the impression that the enemies' swords were already raised and ready to fall. (Note, too, that it is called "the king's command and edict" here. In contrast to Esther's diplomacy in 8:5, the narrator does not take any pains to shield him from responsibility.) At this climactic moment, the tables unexpectedly turn, and the anticipated day of defeat turns into a day of victory for the Jews. One cannot help but recall all of the other reversals of fortune in the book. Yet it seems the author has saved the most sweeping one until last.

Significantly, the words used to describe the victory are the same ones used in both edicts (3:13; 8:11). In verse 5 the Jews are described as "slaughtering" (*hereg*; elsewhere translated as "kill") and "destroying" (*ʾabdān*) those who hated them (see also vv. 6, 7, 12, 15, and 16). One wonders if it is significant that "annihilate" (*šāmad*) is left out. Perhaps it is omitted to show some measure of self-restraint on the part of the Jews (though this may be canceled out by the phrase in v. 5 that says they "did as they pleased to those who hated them").

Still, some significant elements of restraint are evident. The suggestion that they did not kill women and children has already been argued (see pp. 74–75). Most obvious, however, is the fact that they refrained from touching any plunder. This is clearly a matter of some sensitivity to the narrator, since it is repeated three times (vv. 10, 15, and 16). In light of the lingering feelings about the Agag debacle, this detail may have seemed especially important (see 1 Sam. 15 and above, p. 36). With the triumph of Saul's descendant, Mordecai, over Agag's descendant, Haman, this unhappy chapter in Israelite memory may finally reach some closure.

The killing of Haman's ten sons deserves special attention. Notice that they are not, in fact, executed. Rather, they are killed (*hārag*) in the general melee, which would imply that they were among the attackers. More will be said in a moment about the fate of their corpses. For now, however, suffice to say that the list of their names is singled out in the narrative, as if to underscore the fact that—in contrast to Agag—no one would be left to carry on Haman's hateful legacy.

Ahasuerus's response to the news that five hundred of his subjects have been killed in the capital city alone is astonishingly philosophical (compare David's "the sword devours now one and now another" in 2 Sam. 11:25). While we might understand his having mixed emotions about the whole affair, his eagerness to report the news and his casual curiosity about the death toll in the provinces seems at least a little callous (v. 12a). Still, we can hardly be too critical, since a happy ending depends on his support. There is a brief moment of tension in the narrative when we wonder whether his famous anger will flare again (see 1:12 and 7:7–10). We cannot be sure how he will react to the news of a Persian defeat until he speaks.

The second part of Ahasuerus's response is even more astonishing. Without even waiting for Esther to ask, he offers to fulfill another request. "Now what is your petition?" he asks helpfully. "It shall be granted you. And what further is your request? It shall be fulfilled" (12b). Missing is the invitation to give her up to half his kingdom, but perhaps he thinks it goes without saying since they have rehearsed this drill so many times (5:3, 6; 7:2). Missing, too, is any mention of the all-important scepter. The royal relationship seems much relaxed in this scene. Even Esther pares down the preliminaries, prefacing her request with a simple "If it pleases the king" (v. 13). It is hard to believe that this accommodating king is the same one who inspired such fear and trembling in earlier scenes. Perhaps he, too, has been infected with the "dread" that is leading so many of his subjects to support the Jews (cf. 8:17; 9:3).

Esther's request for a second day to continue the killing requires careful consideration. In the first part of her response to Ahasuerus, she asks that "the Jews who are in Susa be allowed tomorrow to do according to this day's edict" (v. 13a). Throughout the centuries, Christian commentators have seized on this as being unforgivably bloodthirsty. Yet it could also be construed as wise. Reflect on the following.

Notice, first, that she expressly asks that the first day's edict be extended for a second day. This means that the same rules and restrictions will apply. The Jews will not be initiating random attacks, in other words, but defending themselves against those who attack them and their families.

Also notice that she responds without hesitation. This is reminiscent of Haman's quick response to the king's question about what should be done for the man the king wishes to honor (6:6–9). The alacrity with which they respond leads one to suspect that they have already given the matter some thought. Yet why would Esther have given this possibility any thought?

It may be relevant that her request is limited to Susa and not to all the surrounding provinces. Reports from the provinces have not yet come in, so she has no knowledge of what has happened there. She does have knowledge of the success—and hence the level of resistance—closer to home. Could it be that the same people who provided the intelligence about the number of Persians killed also brought news of the number of hostile attackers remaining? This would be pure speculation except for the fact that when the Jews of Susa are granted an additional day to defend themselves, three hundred more are killed (v. 15). This would seem to indicate that there were still plenty of enemies out there waiting to mount an attack.

In light of the above considerations it seems patently unfair to characterize Esther as "bloodthirsty." Her request is completely consistent with her character as we have seen it develop in the rest of the book. She is an extremely intelligent leader, able to take the measure of her enemies and anticipate their attack. Her concern is for the safety of her people. Under the circumstances, the fact that she does not ask for a second day in the provinces as well shows remarkable restraint.

The second half of her request has been equally maligned. In the last half of verse 13, she asks that the bodies of the ten sons of Haman be hanged upon the gallows (or, as discussed in chap. 5, impaled upon stakes; see p. 55). This, too, seems unaccountably vicious to most modern readers. The public display—and thus, disgrace—of an enemy's body was not at all unusual in the ancient world, however. Such was the fate of Saul and his sons, for instance, in 1 Samuel 31:8–10. (Could there be some symmetry at work here with regard to the Agag/Saul story?) Esther's act is, in the words of one astute observer, a "shot over the bow," designed to discourage others who might try to imitate their treachery. It also sends an unambiguous message that Haman's cause has no future. So again, the second part of her request is completely in line with her concern for the safety of her people.

At last, the reports come in from the provinces (vv. 16–17). Notice once more the emphasis on self-defense and refraining from plunder. The number of those killed is staggering (75,000), but one must remember the tendency toward exaggeration throughout the book. What looms largest about this statistic is that it reveals the vast number of "those who hated them," and hence, the vast extent of the threat. No wonder the Jews of the provinces rested on the fourteenth day and made it a day of "feasting and gladness." The celebrations are reminiscent of those on the banks of the Red Sea when Miriam and her sisters take up the tambourines, dancing and singing in praise for their deliverance from the Egyptians (Exod. 15:20–21). Psalm 149 gives voice to similar emotions, praising the God who "adorns the humble with victory" (v. 4).

Verses 18 and 19 pause to describe the celebrations of the Jews in Susa, which were dated differently from those of the Jews in the surrounding provinces. Still fighting for their lives on the fourteenth day of Adar, they do not get to rest until the fifteenth. In addition to the requisite gladness and feasting, verse 19 includes the detail of their sending "gifts of food to one another." Although this may seem insignificant, it points to a spirit of generosity that is important for understanding the nature of the celebration. The experience of receiving God's grace begets more grace. Centuries later another Jew named Paul would describe it this way: "Yes, everything is for your sake, so that grace, as it extends to more and more people, may increase thanksgiving, to the glory of God" (2 Cor. 4:15).

Esther 9:20–10:3
Lest We Forget

The remainder of chapter 9 is devoted to the establishment of the festival of Purim, named, of course, after the plural "pur" cast by Haman to determine the day of the Jews' demise (3:7; 9:24). It should be noted that even the name of this festival calls attention to the "great reversal" at the end of the book, in which a day of defeat became, by the grace of God, a day of salvation.

Verses 20 through 23 describe Mordecai's role in establishing and perpetuating the festival "as the days on which the Jews gained relief from their enemies, and as the month that had been turned for them from sorrow into gladness and from mourning into a holiday." Mention is made again of the gifts of food that are to be exchanged, but in addition, this passage talks of "presents to the poor." This concern for the poor runs like a red thread through both testaments, but here we can see how closely connected it is to the impulse to give from what one has received. It makes perfect sense that the exiles of Esther, so recently weak and poor themselves, should want to commemorate their salvation with gestures of generosity (see also Deut. 5:12–15; 10:19).

Scholars have long suspected that the material in this section of the

81

book (9:20–10:3) may be secondary in nature, that is, from a different source and added at a later date. Verses 24 and following certainly reflect a different perspective. There is some overlap in vocabulary (note especially the use of the word "devised" in v. 25) and content, but the story line differs in a couple of important respects.

Perhaps it is simply that the summary in verses 24 and following is "streamlined," but Ahasuerus seems to assume much more of the credit in this version. Mordecai disappears from the story altogether in verse 25, for instance, along with the second edict! Instead, Esther comes before the king, who then gives

> orders in writing that the wicked plot that [Haman] had devised against the Jews should come upon his own head, and that he and his sons should be hanged on the gallows.

This description makes it sound as if Ahasuerus simply dashed off a memo, single-handedly dispatching both Haman and his sons. While this may have been more along the lines of what Esther had in mind when she made her request, it is not the same story that forms the subject matter of all of chapter 8 and most of chapter 9. No mention is made of the king's inability to retract the first edict, and hence, there is no need for a second one. (In fact, one cannot even be sure that there is a *first* edict, given the nebulous reference to "the wicked plot that he had devised against the Jews.") The result is that the resolution of the plot depends not on Esther and Mordecai's quick thinking or the Jews' own acts of self-defense, but on Ahasuerus coming in to save the day. While it is true that he triumphs through a written order, this does not clearly correspond with anything in particular in the earlier version of the story (though it may overlap with the "decree" of 9:14).

This rather more flattering portrayal of Ahasuerus characterizes this whole section (9:24–10:3). Not only is he credited with saving the Jews from Haman's plot, but his acts of "power and might" are extolled with an exuberance that is at least vaguely reminiscent of chapter 1. Chapter 10, verse 1 even rhapsodizes about his tax plan!

Still, Mordecai does receive considerable attention here, even if it is of a different kind from what we might expect. He is recognized primarily for his role in establishing and perpetuating the festival of Purim (which is, indeed, the major focus of the end of the book). Instead of two edicts, the emphasis here in the epilogue is on two letters, both having to do with the Purim festival. In the final form of the text Mordecai is given full credit for the first one (9:20–23, already discussed above). He shares credit with Esther for the second, which is described in 9:29–32.

If Mordecai's role is diminished in the epilogue, then Esther's is diminished even more. She does make a brief appearance in verse 25, where her role in the deliverance is reduced to "but when Esther came before the king." She then disappears until the letter-writing campaign in 9:29–32. There is good reason to believe that this "second letter" may originally have been Esther's alone—a kind of counterpart to Mordecai's first mass mailing in 9:20–23 (cf. v. 26). The phrase "along with the Jew Mordecai, gave full written authority" is described as "dubious" in the textual note corresponding to this verse in the Hebrew Bible (BHS). If we look carefully, we can see why. The verb "to write" with which the Hebrew verse begins is in the third-person feminine singular ("she wrote"). Thus, a literal translation of the verse without the parenthetical material about Mordecai would read, "And Queen Esther daughter of Abihail wrote . . . this second letter about Purim." There then follows the description in verse 30 of the gist of this second round of letters. It would appear, then, that Mordecai's name and imprimatur might have been appended to the text at some point, possibly in an attempt to bolster the authenticity of Esther's letter.

This is not to suggest that we strike out the part about Mordecai in our English Bibles. It is, however, to raise the possibility that at some earlier stage of the text, Mordecai was given credit for the first Purim letter and Esther for the second. This would be consistent with the balance between those two characters in the body of the book. In the final form of these verses she is much less visible, even sharing credit of this second Purim letter with her cousin Mordecai, whose confirmation seems to be required even for its sending. Such a "demotion" cannot help but strike the reader as jarring because Esther has been giving most of the orders since the end of chapter 4—even indirectly to the king!

There is a certain irony in the fact that in a passage that places so much emphasis on memory, the story should take a slightly different shape here. Still, the basic outlines of miraculous deliverance remain the same. Although the community of faith may disagree about exactly who should get the credit, there is no argument about the reality of the rescue nor the necessity of remembering it. In language that sounds very like that of Deuteronomy's plea to remember the passover, this passage pleads with us to pass on this story throughout the generations (Deut. 6:12; 20–25).

Christians may wonder whether this plea applies to them, since the church does not celebrate the feast of Purim. We would do well to remember, however, the main event of that celebration: namely, the reading of the book of Esther. Surely, we can manage that much. Indeed, we should more than "manage" it, because there is a sense in which this book may have come into our canon "for just such a time as this" (4:14). It is a book, after all, about the struggle to be faithful in the midst of an increasingly unfaithful culture. It is a story of courage, faith, and deliverance. It is the story of men and women working together with a God who is not always obvious, but who is always gracious. In sum, it is a powerful word for the present . . . made even more powerful for its being written down.

Yet, as the book itself reminds us in the story about Ahasuerus's sleepless night, a living word is no more than a dead letter if it is not read. Perhaps we should not wait for a sleepless night to read and preach and revel in the book of Esther.

The Apocryphal or Deuterocanonical Additions to Esther

INTRODUCTION

1. The Placement of the Additions

Protestants are often surprised by the presence of six additional sections to the book of Esther in Roman Catholic and Eastern Orthodox versions of the Bible. Sometimes these extra verses (107 in all) are printed between the Old and New Testaments along with the other "apocryphal" (Roman Catholics prefer the term "deuterocanonical") books. Other times, they are printed just after the commonly held version of Esther. If one were to look at a translation of the Septuagint (that is, the Greek translation of the Hebrew text of the Old Testament), one would find the additions interspersed throughout the book of Esther, according to the place they most logically "fit."

The explanation behind this puzzling variety of printing decisions is not as complex as one might expect. It begins with the story of the text (or texts) of the book of Esther that have been handed down throughout the centuries.

The earliest Hebrew manuscripts of the book of Esther did not include these additional verses. (For more detail, see Carey Moore, *Daniel, Esther, and Jeremiah: The Additions*, 153–54.) Yet they are a part of the Greek Septuagint, a translation of the Hebrew Bible made for Greek-speaking Jews in the second or first century B.C.E.

When Jerome set about translating the Bible into Latin in the late fourth century C.E., he took note of the fact that these additions were not part of the Hebrew text and decided to place them *after* his translation of the rest of the book. This decision accounts for the fact that the additions are printed "out of sequence," but at the end of the book in some Bibles.

85

At the time of the Reformation, Protestants were becoming increasingly uncomfortable with recognizing the full canonical authority of many of the books now designated as apocryphal or deuterocanonical. This discomfort is reflected in a Dutch Bible published in Antwerp in 1526 by Jacob van Liesveldt. This edition was the first to print these writings as a separate section between the Old and New Testaments. By 1599, Geneva Bibles were being printed that excluded the books altogether (though ironically, they were still listed in the table of contents). The King James Version of 1611 was published both with and without the apocryphal/deuterocanonical books. (For more detail, see Carol Newsom's essay "Introduction to the Apocryphal/Deuterocanonical Books," in the third edition of the *New Oxford Annotated Bible, NRSV with the Apocrypha*.)

This short history, then, accounts for the many and various ways that these disputed books—and more specifically, the additions to Esther—are printed in modern Bibles. But what do the additions contain, and what might have motivated people to add them?

2. The Nature of the Additions

Most of the additions to Esther occur in six clusters, now helpfully labeled A, B, C, D, E, and F. Earlier practices of trying to assign chapter and verse numbers to the additions are quite confusing, especially since there is so little agreement as to their placement. Nevertheless, reference is made to the Vulgate's system of identification in order to clarify the points of correspondence.

The nature of the major additions may be summarized as follows:

Addition A—Located before 1:1
Mordecai dreams of troubling times to come (Vulgate 11:2–12)
Mordecai uncovers the plot of the two eunuchs and is rewarded by the king (Vulgate 12:1–6)
Addition B—Located after 3:13
The text of Haman's edict against the Jews (Vulgate 13:1–7)
Addition C—Located after 4:17
Mordecai prays for deliverance (Vulgate 13:8–18)
Esther prays for courage and deliverance (Vulgate 14:1–19)
Addition D—Located after 4:17 and Addition C; replaces 5:1–2
Esther approaches the king (Vulgate 15:4–19)
Addition E—Located after 8:12
The text of Mordecai's edict in defense of the Jews (Vulgate 16:1–24)
Addition F—Located after 10:3
Mordecai interprets his dream (Vulgate 10:4–13)
A final inscription (Vulgate 1:11)

In addition to these major clusters, there are a few additional phrases, sprinkled throughout the Septuagint's version of the book, that also merit some attention. In 2:20, for instance, the phrase "to fear God and keep his laws" is added to the description of Esther's upbringing by Mordecai. In 4:8, the phrase "call upon the Lord" fills out Mordecai's instructions to Esther with regard to Haman's decree. The phrase "That night the Lord took sleep from the king" in 6:1 makes it clear that Ahasuerus's insomnia is no accident. Finally, Zeresh's vaguely ominous words about Haman's downfall are rendered chillingly precise with the addition of "because the living God is with him" (6:13).

There is general agreement among scholars that these additions were not written at the same time. The fact that Josephus paraphrased B, C, D, and E in 93 C.E. pinpoints that date as the latest possible for the composition of those additions. Additions A and F were evidently part of the Hebrew text translated by Lysimachus in the late second to early first century B.C.E. (see Addition F:1). There is also considerable suspicion that while A, C, D, and F were originally composed in either Hebrew or Aramaic, additions B and E were almost certainly composed in Greek. In any case, all of the additions eventually found their way into the Septuagint's text of Esther.

3. The Character of the Additions

Even though the additions may have been composed in separate circumstances, taken together they alter the book of Esther in some significant ways. Several general observations may be made in this regard.

It is said that nature abhors a vacuum. The same could be said for the additions to the book of Esther.

As was obvious from the description of the "minor" additions above, one of the reasons for the additions is the perceived absence of God in this book (see Introduction, pp. 13–14). While the name of God is noticeably absent in the Hebrew version of Esther, references to God abound in the additions (there are more than fifty). The overall effect of these insertions is to magnify the religious quality of the book. More specifically, the insertion of these references affects our impression of both the human characters and the divine character. For instance, both Mordecai and Esther offer eloquent, passionate prayers to God in Addition C, thus establishing their piety in a much more overt way than the Hebrew text does. Still more significantly, in the Greek version God's character comes screaming out from behind the scenes. God is the stated cause for the king's insomnia in 6:1 and is given full credit for "chang[ing] the spirit of the king to gentleness" in D:8. While the Hebrew left us to wonder over such "coincidences," the Greek makes

God's agency explicit, thus filling in the "vacuum" of suggestion with the substance of certainty.

Closely related to the overt references to God are the overt references to Jewish dietary and ethical concerns. Esther's prayer in Addition C fills in what many feel to be the deafening silence of the Hebrew version, as she expresses her disgust at having to endure her Gentile diet, her Gentile wealth, and her Gentile husband. If we had any doubts about her religious sincerity, the addition puts them to rest.

One of the most notorious ellipses of the Hebrew version has to do with Mordecai's motivation when he refuses to bow down to Haman in chapter 3. Again, the Greek Addition C removes all ambiguity by filling in the blank with an explanation. "I did this," Mordecai tells God in his prayer in C:14, "so that I might not set human glory above the glory of God."

Whoever wrote Additions A and F must have held an apocalyptic view of the world. As Newsom points out, the addition of Mordecai's dream and its interpretation frame the story in a new way, and "graft onto it a new apocalyptic perspective of cosmic struggle between good and evil" (54).

Some of the so-called vacuums in the Hebrew version are not so much logical or even theological, but theatrical. This seems to be the case with Addition D, which describes Esther's unauthorized appearance before the king in dramatic (melodramatic?) fashion. One gets the sense that the relatively terse description of the Hebrew was simply too much for the author of this addition, who could not resist playing the scene for all it was worth. Some have suggested that the high drama of D actually shifts the climax of the book away from 7:5 ("this evil man Haman!") to Esther's deliverance from Ahasuerus's "fierce anger" (D:7) (see Newsom, 54; also Levenson, 30).

Finally, Additions B and E fill in a blank by supplying the texts of the two all-important edicts—Haman's, which orders the destruction of the Jews, and Mordecai's, which authorizes their right to self-defense. This type of interpolation is not at all unusual in ancient literature; we have only to look to Ezra 1:2–4 and 4:11–22 for examples even within the canon. Levenson notes that Additions B and E enhance—or at least attempt to enhance—"the annalistic nature of the MT's style and lend more credibility to the tale" (31).

This is obviously not all that could be said about the character of the additions to Esther. Yet these brief observations do point out a pattern, namely, the additions' tendency to supply something their authors thought to be lacking in the Hebrew version of the story. Some have felt that they did not, in fact, do the book any favors by "filling in the blank."

Others greet their contributions with delight and relief. The difference is often determined by how comfortable one is with ambiguity. It may also reflect whether one prefers subtlety or clarity.

4. The Status of the Additions

Finally, the status of the additions to Esther is not determined by how one feels about them either literarily or theologically. Neither is it determined by their "secondary" nature, that is, their being written later than the rest of the book. (If this were the sole criterion for authority, a significant percentage of the canon would not make the cut.) In the last analysis, canonical status is determined by one's community of faith. As described above, different communities of faith have made different decisions about these additional verses. It is to be hoped that the above reflections on the placement, nature, and character of the additions, as well as the more specific comments that follow, will deepen our respect for each other, and enhance our ability to appreciate both versions of the book of Esther.

COMMENTARY

1. Addition A:1–17 (Located before 1:1)

The first part of this addition (A:1–11; Vulgate 1:2–12) narrates Mordecai's dream of troubling times to come. It begins, necessarily, with an introduction, since Mordecai does not make an appearance in the Hebrew version until chapter 2. As well as rendering the later introduction redundant, the addition puts an interpretive spin on Mordecai's genealogy. In our discussion of the Hebrew text of chapter 2 (p. 30), we noted that the syntax of 2:5–6 is elastic enough to allow either Mordecai or his grandfather, Kish, to be the one who was carried off into exile. The addition resolves the syntactical problem, but compounds the logistical one, stating that it was indeed Mordecai who had been taken captive. As was pointed out in the main commentary, this would make Mordecai well over one hundred years old at the time of the story.

Mordecai's biography is not the focus of the addition, however. Rather, his dream of two great dragons (Haman and Mordecai?) takes center stage. As these dragons prepare to fight, all the nations of the earth prepare to go to war against "the righteous nation." These contests are set against a background of cosmic chaos. In language echoing the special effects so typical of apocalyptic literature, A:5 describes "noises and confusion, thunders and earthquake" (see Isa. 24:17–20; Joel 2:10). The righteous are understandably afraid and cry out to God for aid. It comes in the form of a "tiny spring" that is transformed into a "great river" (Esther?). This vision ends with the victory of the right-

89

eous, depicted with images of the now exalted lowly devouring those who had been held in honor previously. Not surprisingly, this dream gives Mordecai a lot to think about, and the addition notes that he has it "on his mind, seeking all day to understand it in every detail" (A:11).

As we seek to understand it, at least three things become clear. First, this dream, along with its interpretive counterpart in Addition F, reframes the story of Esther and attempts to establish apocalyptic as the literary genre. That this significantly affects the reader's expectations hardly requires comment. Second, it makes God's agency in what follows indisputable. A:11 (Addition A; Vulgate 11:12) says, "Mordecai saw in this dream what God had determined to do. . . ." There is a sense in which God thus becomes the main character of the book (with Mordecai a close second and Esther the "tiny spring" perhaps a distant third). Finally, the shift toward cosmic consequences significantly raises the stakes of the story. Now we not only have to worry about Esther and Mordecai as individuals, and the Jews as a people, but all creation in the bargain.

The second part of Addition A (A:12–17; Vulgate 12:1–6) tells the story of how Mordecai overhears two eunuchs, Gabatha and Thara, plotting to assassinate the king (called Artaxerxes throughout the Greek text). He informs the king, and the would-be assassins are summarily executed. The king records the incident and rewards Mordecai by ordering him to serve in the court. The vignette concludes by noting that Haman "determined to injure Mordecai and his people because of the two eunuchs of the king" (A:17; Vulgate 12:6).

At first, this story seems clumsy and out of place, since it renders the description of the same incident in 2:21–23 redundant. Given the fact that the names of the two eunuchs are similar (Gabatha and Tharra in Addition A; Bigthan and Teresh in 2:21), we might well write off the inconsistency of their names as a result of difficulties in transmission or translation. Besides, why would one want two stories about the same thing in one book?

Yet, on closer examination, we cannot be sure that this passage *does* describe the same incident as the one in 2:21–23. The names of the eunuchs, after all, are different. And considering the addition as a separate incident does resolve some possible tensions within the Hebrew text by providing extra information. First, it explains how Mordecai rose to such prominence in the Persian court. Second, it explains the antipathy between Haman and Mordecai. Third, it suggests that Haman supported the foiled assassination attempt, making his character even more sinister. Perhaps the author of this segment of Addition A thought that these "bonuses" were worth giving readers a sense of déjà vu when encountering a very similar story in chapter 2.

2. Addition B (After 3:13)

This addition (B:1–7; Vulgate 13:1–7) purports to be the text of the edict that Haman writes in the king's name, calling for the destruction of the Jews. Scholars have long noted that the florid style of the Greek in this addition (and its counterpart, Addition E) suggests that it was indeed written in Greek and is not based on a Hebrew or Aramaic original. In any case, its extravagant style fits well with what we have come to expect from the Persian court in the rest of the Hebrew version. One would hardly expect Haman (or Ahasuerus/Artaxerxes) to communicate in simple, self-effacing prose.

One of the things this addition contributes is an appearance of verisimilitude. The Hebrew version puts great emphasis on this edict (understandably), and the Greek addition helpfully supplies the authentic text. Now the readers need not settle for "the hearing of the ear," but our eyes can actually see the original. As was noted above, this type of authenticating insertion is a well-known feature of ancient writing.

The addition also has the effect of further illustrating Haman's inflated ego. Even though the edict is written as if Ahasuerus is speaking, the Hebrew context makes it clear that Haman is, in fact, its author (3:11–12). Thus, when the king heaps praises on his trusty servant, Haman, it is really Haman who is heaping praises on himself. Phrases like "our second father" hint that Haman's ambitions are at least as big as his ego.

The edict also expands on Haman's stated rationale for destroying the Jews (though this, remember, is only a ruse for his personal resentment of Mordecai). The rationale as it is stated in 3:8 is so spare that it is hard to believe the king falls for it. With the addition of the edict, it is as if this is the version of the story Haman has crafted once he has had more time to think about it. Or it may give the impression that what was described earlier was actually a kind of "shorthand" for this, the longer and more convincing version.

This addition has some negative effects, however. There is a glaring inconsistency, for instance, in the date of the anticipated pogrom. The Hebrew, of course, identifies it as being set for the *thirteenth* day of the month of Adar, while the addition specifies the *fourteenth* day. Although the Hebrew version later expands the crucial dates to include the thirteenth *and* the fourteenth days (9:18), this addition offers no explanation to account for the inconsistency.

91

Another possibly negative effect is due to the edict's very convincing use of the first person. Although the Hebrew context does make clear that the king did *not* write this edict, the fact that the entire addition (with the exception of its introductory phrase) is written in the king's own voice may weaken one of the most subtle—but powerful—features of the Hebrew version. As the commentary on chapters 3 and 7 points out, the Hebrew revels in the possibility that the king may be confused about whether he has ordered the Jews to be destroyed or enslaved. The very convincing and extended use of the first person in this addition tends to eclipse that ambiguity, giving the impression that the king knows full well what he is doing. In the Hebrew it is much less clear that he does.

3. Addition C (After 4:17)

Addition C:1–11 (Vulgate 13:8–18) records Mordecai's prayer as he reflects on his own role in his people's predicament and anticipates Esther's uninvited appearance before the king.

One of the most intriguing ellipses in the Hebrew version has to do with Mordecai's motivation for refusing to bow to Haman. The only possible explanations offered in the Hebrew come to us with all the force of a hint. Haman's abrupt promotion on the heels of Mordecai's heroic deflection of the assassination plot *may* suggest some level of personal resentment. This, however, is never spelled out in the text and is left for the reader to infer. The only other possibility is even more mercurial. That is that Mordecai's refusal is rooted in the ancient antipathy between the house of Saul and the house of Benjamin. (For more detail, see our discussion of chap. 3:1–2.)

Thanks to the content of Mordecai's prayer, however, such speculations become moot. As the addition tells using Mordecai's voice,

> it was not in insolence or pride or for any love of glory that I did this, and refused to bow down to this proud Haman; for I would have been willing to kiss the soles of his feet to save Israel! But I did this so that I might not set human glory above the glory of God, and I will not bow down to anyone but you, who are my Lord; and I will not do these things in pride. (C:5b–7; Vulgate 13:12–14)

Thus with one stroke, the addition dispels our doubts about Mordecai's motives and establishes him as a man of extraordinary piety (since it was not, after all, forbidden for Jews to bow down to other people; see Ruth 2:10 and elsewhere). Levenson points out that Mordecai's intense religious scrupulosity on this point raises his actions "into the praiseworthy category of resistance to idolatry, a pressing issue in late Second Temple literature" (84; see, for example, Dan. 3:17–18 and 4:22–24).

Mordecai goes on to remind God, in good prophetic fashion, that it would really be in God's best interest to deliver the Jews (compare Moses' rhetoric in Exod. 32:12, for instance). Mordecai very effectively reminds God that "the inheritance that has been yours from the beginning" is now being threatened. The prayer concludes with a continuation of this rhetorical line, this time echoing the psalms. "Turn our mourning into feasting that we may live and sing praise to your name, O Lord; do not destroy the lips of those who praise you" (compare Psalm 30:9–12).

As if on cue, C:11 tells us that "all Israel cried out mightily, for their death was before their eyes." The effect of this description is threefold. First, it intensifies the drama by making the pain of the people's situation that much more vivid. Second, it moves the attention away from Mordecai and acts as a transition to what follows. Third, this poignant description of the people's reaction suggests that the people have actually been present for Mordecai's prayer. If this is so, then they have "overheard" Mordecai's self-defense in the early part of the prayer. Cynical readers may suspect that Mordecai was actually counting on this, and was thus playing to two "audiences."

Addition C:12–30 (Vulgate 14:1–19) describes Esther's preparation for her interview with the king and relates the contents of her prayer. Esther's death is apparently "before her eyes" as well, since the text says she is "seized with deadly anxiety." While the Hebrew version records her intention for a three-day fast in preparation (4:16), it leaves the details of this to our imagination. Chapter 5 then opens with her donning the royal robes and setting off for the throne room. Addition C not only tells us how she feels in the interim, but also describes her taking off the royal robes and replacing them with "garments of distress and mourning." Perfume is exchanged for "ashes and dung" until her body is "utterly humbled." The description sums up by saying that "every part that she loved to adorn she covered with her tangled hair." One gets the impression that the effects of her yearlong beauty treatment (2:12) have been undone in a matter of minutes.

When one compares Esther's prayer with that of Mordecai in the preceding section, there are many overlaps. If one looks broadly at the content of both, there is a kind of thematic chiasmus. Mordecai begins by protesting his innocence and ends with a passionate plea for the people's salvation. The first half of Esther's prayer is weighted with prayers for her people, while the last half is devoted to assertions of personal innocence. As with Mordecai's prayer, Esther's assertions fill in some of the blanks in the Hebrew version of the tale. While the Hebrew only hints at how Esther might have felt about her new life in the palace, the Greek leaves no doubt about her revulsion at "the splendor of the wicked," "the bed of the uncircumcised," and the non-kosher table of both Haman and the king. Her most graphic rejection is reserved for her crown, which she says she abhors "like a filthy (i.e., menstruous) rag." So much for subtlety!

4. *Addition D* (*After 4:17 and Addition C; replaces 5:1–2*)

Addition D begins by describing another change of clothes, as Esther readies herself for the royal audience. The robes of mourning and humility are once again exchanged for the "splendid attire" of the court—so splendid, in fact, that she is "radiant with perfect beauty."

Esther's personal transformation corresponds to the stylistic transformation that results when the Hebrew 5:1–2 is replaced with Addition D. Drama is exchanged for melodrama, as the simple (albeit dangerous) act of walking into the throne room is adorned with vivid detail. Instead of walking into the inner court alone, Esther here walks with two maids, leaning on the one for support while the other brings up the rear, carrying her train. (This second maid is probably more than ornamental, since the train of such splendid attire could well have been quite heavy. There is a sense in which both maids are there to help Esther bear the burden of both her weight and her responsibility.) Instead of an instant's uncertainty about the king's response, the addition spreads the suspense out over several verses, complete with fainting spells and gallant clichés ("Speak to me").

A theological transformation occurs as well. God's participation in the Hebrew version is so subtle as to be almost invisible. Unless one counts the "coincidence" of Esther's catching the king's eye from the court, there is precious little evidence of God's agency. We are not told why the king holds out the golden scepter; we are simply told that he does. The addition, however, leaves little doubt about who is pulling the strings in this scene. The miracle is set up with a description of the king's "fierce anger," which is so intense that one look causes the queen to faint. Our hopes are fainting with her when God steps in to save the day, "chang[ing] the spirit of the king to gentleness."

Lastly, there is a climactic transformation in the addition. The high drama of this scene essentially upstages the climax of the Hebrew story. In the Hebrew, we are *reassured* by the king's favorable response in chapter 5, but we are by no means *sure* that it will last. The tension builds until Esther finally makes her request in chapter 7 and reveals

94

Haman's true colors. The climax comes when the king finally condemns him to death. In the addition, however, we are so electrified by Esther's personal peril, so relieved by God's timely rescue, and so convinced of the king's subsequent goodwill that the rest of the story reads like the denouement it now is.

There are a couple of delightful continuities between Addition D and the Hebrew, however, and they have to do with Esther's character. At first, the swooning queen of the addition seems to have little in common with the dignified queen of the earlier version. Yet both of them struggle to put on a brave front, and much of both narratives' tension derives from the tension between the internal and the external Esther. Both are possessed of a certain presence of mind as well. This grace under pressure is not as obvious in the Esther of the addition, but it is there nonetheless. After fainting from what is probably a combination of both fear and hunger, she refers to neither in the explanation she gives to the king. Perhaps she is being sincere when she tells him that she saw him "like an angel of God" and was overwhelmed by his "glory," but given what she said about him in her prayer, one has reason to doubt it. If she's not sincere, then it means she is pretty savvy, and thus at least a close cousin to her counterpart in the Hebrew version of the story.

5. Addition E *(After 8:12)*

Addition E:1–24 (Vulgate 16:1–24) supplies the text of Mordecai's edict in defense of the Jews. Like its counterpart in Addition B, this wordy edict is written in the name and with the voice of the king. It goes beyond the Hebrew story in at least three significant ways.

First, the edict that Mordecai dictates in 8:9ff. allows the Jews to defend themselves from the anticipated attack on the thirteenth of Adar. While the text of the addition's edict does this as well, it spends more time defending the king than it does defending the Jews. The first sixteen verses of Addition E are devoted to helping Artaxerxes save face. Since the first edict praised Haman to the skies, this one must grind his reputation into the ground. He is described as a "thrice-accursed man" who has conspired against innocent, upstanding citizens (i.e., the Jews), plotted to kill Mordecai and Esther, and attempted to overthrow the king. Worst of all, he is a foreigner (this, remember, was one of the "crimes" of which he accused the Jews), and an ungrateful one at that. While this extended self-justification may seem like a ridiculous digression, it is perhaps necessitated by both the fact of the first edict and the first-person approach to both. How, after all, would a king save face in a situation like this? The imaginative author of Addition E shows us.

This edict also goes beyond its canonical counterpart in urging loyal Persian subjects to refrain from attacking the Jews at all. "You will therefore do well not to put in execution the letters sent by Haman son of Hammedatha," he warns in E:17 (Vulgate 16:17), pointing out that the author of said letters has since "been hanged at the gate of Susa with all his household." This order is, in essence, what Esther and Mordecai hoped for in the Hebrew version but could not get, that is, an edict that would in some way rescind the first one (8:5). Although this section of the addition may fall short of a full revocation, it packs considerably more punch than Ahasuerus's flat refusal in 8:8.

Lastly, the king in Addition E is surprisingly pious. He sprinkles his edict with confessional language about God (E:4, 16, 21). He even gives God the credit for Haman's execution (E:18). But most significant, he actually seems to anticipate the establishment of Purim and enjoins the Persians to join in too (E:21–23)! Even if we grant that it is Mordecai who is ghostwriting the edict, this version of the king sounds like he is ready to convert.

6. Addition F (After 10:3)

Most of Addition F is devoted to decoding Mordecai's dream (see Addition A). F:1–11 (Vulgate 10:4–11:1) records Mordecai's reflections on what has transpired and his attempt to interpret them as a fulfillment of the vision God had given him before the events took place. Esther is identified as the "little spring" that became a "great river." The two dragons who spar and roar are Haman and Mordecai. The terrified "righteous nation" that cries out to God for deliverance is, of course, the Jewish people, who are eventually exalted in both the story and the dream.

As was mentioned in our discussion of Addition A, the character and tenor of both additions are completely in line with apocalyptic literature elsewhere. The only atypical feature is that Mordecai is represented as one of the dragons. As Levenson points out, "dragons tend to represent the primordial and eschatological enemies of God, and not heroes" (135). Yet there may be a sense in which this unusual identification actually echoes some of the ambiguity in Mordecai's character (at least in the Hebrew version of the story). Just as the fighting of the two dragons triggers the nations to make war on the "righteous nation," so Haman and Mordecai's disagreement ignites the danger for the Jews in the story of Esther.

96 The fact that Esther begins as a little spring and grows into a great river may also reflect the Hebrew version more closely. Although both versions depict a young woman of humble origins who becomes the

queen of a nation and a heroine of her people, the Esther of the additions is a much more static character than that of the Hebrew version. The dramatic development of Esther's character in the Hebrew version seems much more in line with the symbolism of Additions A and F. One cannot help but wonder if A and F were added before B through E. This could account for the congruities between the vision and both Esther and Mordecai's characters.

There is less congruity, however, between the "two lots" of Addition F and anything in either the MT of Esther or the other additions. First of all, the lots of Addition F do not correspond to anything in the dream of Addition A. Second, F:7's (Vulgate 10:10) interpretation of these lots as representing "the people of God" and "the nations" seems to be strangely at odds with the Hebrew version's singular "lot" (pur vs. purim) which is cast in 3:7 to determine the date for Haman's pogrom. Still, the symbolic interpretation seems to give way in even the addition itself, when reference is made to the observance of the fourteenth and fifteenth of Adar. This, at least, aligns the addition more closely with 9:26's reference to "Purim."

It may be a mistake to get too bogged down in precise correspondences, however. It is, after all, part of the nature of apocalyptic to be multivalent. Perhaps we would do well to follow the advice of one teacher of the book of Revelation who advised his students, "Visualize, don't analyze." When we lose ourselves in the vision that now brackets the book of Esther, we are sure of only one thing: "these things have come from God" (F:1). That may be all we need to know for sure.

The last word in the apocryphal/deuterocanonical additions to Esther comes from an anonymous librarian. Addition F:11 (Vulgate 11:1) is a "colophon," that is, an inscription appended to the end of a manuscript. This one describes the date, process, and people responsible for the manuscript's translation and transport. Although the date seems to be precise ("in the fourth year of the reign of Ptolemy and Cleopatra"), it is rendered less so by the fact that there are several Ptolemies married to Cleopatras. (Most scholars seem to prefer the pair who reigned around 114 B.C.E.) One "Lysimachus, son of Ptolemy, one of the residents of Jerusalem" is given credit for the translation (though we cannot be sure about the exact shape of the text he translated). Someone named "Dositheus, who said that he was a priest and a Levite, and his son Ptolemy brought to Egypt the preceding letter about Purim, which they said was authentic."

Perhaps the most important conclusion we can draw from this colophon is that its author thought it was important to attest in whatever way he could to the authenticity of what he calls "the preceding letter about Purim." His passion attests to the presence of a living community of faith that valued the book he had received. In a sense, it is appropriate that this Appendix should end with such a reference. Even if we do not know exactly what his version of the book of Esther looked like, we can be sure that there was a living community of faith who saw it as the word of God for them. Whatever our version of the book of Esther looks like, we must do likewise.

BIBLIOGRAPHY

For Further Study

Childs, Brevard S. "Esther." *Introduction to the Old Testament as Scripture*. Philadelphia: Fortress Press, 1979.

Clines, David J. A. "The Esther Scroll: The Story of the Story." In *Journal for the Study of the Old Testament*, Supplement Series 30. Sheffield: JSOT Press, 1984.

Craig, Kenneth. *Reading Esther: A Case for the Literary Carnivalesque*. Literary Currents in Biblical Interpretation, edited by Danna Nolan Fewell and David M. Gunn. Louisville, Ky.: Westminster John Knox Press, 1995.

Day, Linda. "Three Faces of a Queen: Characterization in the Books of Esther." In *Journal for the Study of the Old Testament*, Supplement Series 186, edited by David J. A. Clines and Philip R. Davies. Sheffield: Sheffield Academic Press, 1995.

Moore, Carey A. *Studies in the Book of Esther*. New York: KTAV Publishing House, 1982.

Niditch, Susan. "Short Stories: The Book of Esther and the Theme of Woman as a Civilizing Force." In *Old Testament Interpretation—Past, Present, and Future: Essays in Honor of Gene M. Tucker*, edited by James L. Mays, David L. Petersen, and Kent H. Richards. Nashville: Abingdon Press, 1995.

Sasson, Jack M. "Esther." In *The Literary Guide to the Bible*, edited by Robert Alter and Frank Kermode. Cambridge, Mass.: Harvard University Press, 1987.

White, Sidnie Ann. "Esther." In *The Women's Bible Commentary*, edited by Carol A. Newsom and Sharon H. Ringe. Louisville, Ky.: Westminster John Knox Press, 1992.

Literature Cited

Baldwin, Joyce G. *Esther*. Tyndale Old Testament Commentaries. Downers Grove, Ill.: Inter-Varsity Press, 1984.

Beal, Timothy K. *Esther*. Berit Olam: Studies in Hebrew Narrative and Poetry. Collegeville, Minn.: Liturgical Press, 1999.

Berg, Sandra Beth. *The Book of Esther: Motifs, Themes and Structure*. Society of Biblical Literature: Dissertation Series. No. 44. Missoula, Mont.: Scholars Press, 1979.

Berlin, Adele. *Esther*. JPS Bible Commentary. Philadelphia: Jewish Publication Society, 2001.

Bickerman, Elias. *Four Strange Books of the Bible*. New York: Schocken Books, 1967.

Bornkamm, Heinrich. *Luther and the Old Testament*. Translated by Eric W. and Ruth C. Gritsch. Mifflintown, Penn.: Sigler Press, 1997.

Brenner, Athalya. "Who's Afraid of Feminist Criticism? Who's Afraid of Biblical Humour? The Case of the Obtuse Foreign Ruler in the Hebrew Bible." *Journal for the Study of the Old Testament* 63 (1994): 38–55.

Consultation on Common Texts. *The Revised Common Lectionary*. Nashville: Abingdon Press, 1992.

Darr, Katheryn Pfisterer. *Far More Precious than Jewels: Perspectives on Biblical Women*. Louisville, Ky.: Westminster/John Knox Press, 1991.

Fox, Michael V. *Character and Ideology in the Book of Esther*. Columbia, S.C.: University of South Carolina Press, 1991.

Gerleman, Gillis. *Esther*. Biblischer Kommentar, Altes Testament 21. Neukirchen-Vluyn: Neukirchener Verlag, 1982.

Herodotus. *The Histories*. Translated by Harry Carter. New York: Heritage Press, 1958.

Levenson, Jon D. *Esther*. The Old Testament Library. Louisville, Ky.: Westminster John Knox Press, 1997.

Lipstadt, Deborah. "No Denying Her Now." *The Jerusalem Post Magazine* (June 2, 2000): 14–16.

Moore, Carey A. *Daniel, Esther, and Jeremiah: The Additions*. Anchor Bible. Garden City, N.Y.: Doubleday & Co., 1977.

———. *Esther*. Anchor Bible. New York: Doubleday, 1971.

Newsom, Carol A. "Introduction to the Apocryphal/Deuterocanonical Books." In *The New Oxford Annotated Bible: New Revised Standard Version with the Apocrypha*, 3d Edition. Michael Coogan, editor. Oxford: Oxford University Press, 2001. Pp. 3–10 in the Apocrypha.

Paton, Lewis Bayles. *The Book of Esther*. International Critical Commentary. New York: Charles Scribner's Sons, 1908.

Radday, Yehuda T. "On Missing the Humour in the Bible." In *On Humour and the Comic in the Hebrew Bible*, edited by Yehuda T. Radday and Athalya Brenner (Sheffield: Almond Press, 1990).

Talmon, Shemaryahu. "'Wisdom' in the Book of Esther." *Vetus Testamentum* 13 (1963): 419–55.

Vrudny, Kimberly. "Medieval Fascination with the Queen: Esther as the Queen of Heaven and Host of the Messianic Banquet." *Arts: The Arts in Religious and Theological Studies* 11/2 (1999): 36–43.

White, Sidnie Ann. "Esther: A Feminine Model for Jewish Diaspora." In *Gender and Difference in Ancient Israel*, edited by Peggy L. Day, 161–77. Minneapolis: Fortress Press, 1989.